Military and Naval Decorations of the United States

Military and Naval Decorations of the United States

Charles P. McDowell

[redacted]
Quest Publishing Company
Post Office Box 2081
Springfield, Virginia 22152

Library of Congresss Cataloging in Publication Data

McDowell, Charles P., 1941-
Military and naval decorations of the United States.

Bibliography:p.
1. United States--Armed Forces--Medals, badges, decorations, etc.
I Title.
UC533.M3 1984 355.1'342'0973 83-83121
ISBN 0-915779-00-5

Contents

Preface ---7
Introduction ---9
Medal of Honor ---15
Brevet Medal ---35
Certificate of Merit ---43
Distinguished Service Cross ---49
Navy Cross ---61
Air Force Cross ---67
Defense Distinguished Service Medal ---71
Army Distinguished Service Medal ---77
Navy Distinguished Service Medal ---81
USAF Distinguished Service Medal ---87
USCG Distinguished Service Medal ---91
Silver Star ---93
Defense Superior Service Medal ---129
Legion of Merit ---133
Distinguished Flying Cross ---139
Lifesaving Medals ---145
Specially Meritorious Service Medal, 1898 ---155
Soldier's Medal ---161
Navy & Marine Corps Medal ---163
Airman's Medal ---167
Coast Guard Medal ---169
Bronze Star Medal ---171

Defense Meritorious Service Medal ------------------------------------175
Meritorious Service Medal --177
Air Medal --181
Joint Service Commendation Medal --------------------------------------185
Navy Commendation Medal --191
Army Commendation Medal --195
USAF Commendation Medal --197
USCG Commendation Medal --199
Joint Service Achievement Medal --203
Navy Achievement Medal ---207
USAF Achievement Medal ---211
Army Achievement Medal ---217
USCG Achievement Medal ---221
Purple Heart Medal --223
Color Plates ---97
Bibliography ---230

PREFACE

In any human enterprise there are always a small number of participants who do more than is expected of them. Nowhere has this been more evident than in the profession of arms. Service in the Armed Forces has always had its unique features, one of which is that it may place the individual in a positon of great danger or may require that he or she work under the most trying of circumstances. Some have faced the horrors of war and risen above them, many giving their lives in the process. "War," as John Stewart Mill once said, "is an ugly thing, but not the ugliest of things. A man who has nothing he cares more about than his personal safety is a miserable creature and has no chance of being free unless made so and kept so by the exertions of better man than himself."

Most military and naval heroes are ordinary people who, when put to the test, rise above all that makes men ordinary and display rare courage, fortitude, and devotion to duty. Afterwards they fade back into the background from which they came. Many of these people are rewarded with decorations -- small bits of cloth and metal which indicate that the person who wears it has done something out of the ordinary.

The idea of using decorations for valor is of ancient vintage. In ancient times the Greeks and Romans used wreaths of various types to signify honor (and many of these wreaths are now symbolically embodied in certain of our military and naval decorations). In the middle ages first the monastic and later the secular orders of knighthood used ornate badges to indicate membership; later these kinds of badges were awarded for acts of merit. The concept was strikingly simple: those who provided some heroic or unique service to the crown or to the state were in effect members of a company of noteworthy individuals, and their membership - based on service or achievement - was to be denoted by the wearing of a medal or badge. Thus emerged the practice of awarding medals for heroism or service.

The United States was formed as a democratic republic, and the notion of badges and symbols was repugnant to the founding fathers who associated such things with what they wished to leave behind when they came to the New World. However, time and circumstances changed this spartan perspective and American heroes (after a few false starts) also came to receive medals as decorations for valor and meritorious achievement. Even at that, American medallic history is relatively new, having its birth in the Civil War and its most rapid growth during the past fifty years.

Unfortunately, little reliable material has been published on American military and naval decorations - a gap which does not correspond to the large and growing interest in the subject. Here, for the first time, is a reference book dedicated to the comprehensive study of American military and naval decorations. The reader will find this book to be historically accurate, up-to-date, and complimented with outstanding photographs of American decorations. This is a long-awaited volume and is a major contribution to the literature on American military and naval awards.

JOHN E. LELLE

Wildwood Crest, New Jersey

January, 1984

INTRODUCTION

In the United States, military and naval decorations as we know them are a relatively recent phenomenon. In the early days of our nation Congress awarded medals; however, they were usually large, bulky, and not intended for wear. They were typically awarded to senior officers for specific military or naval victories and were usually struck in gold; occasionally they were accompanied by a companion medal struck in silver for presentation to subordinate officers. The first of these gold medals was presented to General George Washington and was intended to commemorate the British evacuation of Boston in 1776. These early gold medals were more in the line of tokens of appreciation from Congress to individuals for specific acts of heroism or some notable victory and were not awarded under military authority.

THE ANDRE MEDALS

An interesting variation on the theme of medals from Congress to individuals was the so-called "Andre medals." These medals were awarded to Privates John Paulding, David Williams, and Isaac van Wart, the three young New York State militiamen who captured Major John Andre. Andre, a British spy, had met secretly on the night of September 21, 1780, with Major General Benedict Arnold to complete negotiations for the surrender of the United States garrison at West Point. Andre was subsequently captured and hanged, and Arnold fled to England in disgrace. In gratitude for the disclosure of this plot, Congress enacted a Joint Resolution on November 3, 1780, awarding Paulding, Williams, and van Wart an annual sum of two hundred dollars each and a "silver medal" to be presented "with the thanks of Congress for their fidelity, and the eminent service they have rendered their country." The medals were presented by the Commander in Chief, and although they were presented to soldiers for what might well have been considered a military act, they were not really military decorations in the modern sense.

THE BADGE OF MILITARY MERIT

George Washington was well aware of the sacrifices made by his soldiers and was eager to provide some type of reward for outstanding service. He wanted an award which would be presented by the Commander in Chief and was interested in a decoration which could be awarded to anyone - not just senior officers. As a consequence, on August 7, 1782, he directed that "*Whenever any singularly meritorious action is performed, the author of it shall be permitted to wear on his facings, over his left breast, the figure of a heart in purple cloth, or silk, edged with narrow lace or binding.*"

Although Washington intended for the Badge of Military Merit to be permanent, it fell into disuse after the war. On the two hundredth anniversary of Washington's birth (February 22, 1932), the President directed that the Purple Heart be revived out of respect for Washington's memory and military achievements. The Purple Heart Medal is now awarded for a considerably different reason that Washington had in mind; yet it remains technically our oldest military or naval decoration.

Although the use of medals gained widespread acceptance throughout Europe starting in the middle of the nineteenth century, that was not the case in the United States. One of the major reasons for this can be attributed to the use of "brevet" promotions.

THE RISE OF THE BREVET COMMISSION

Although Congress continued to approve special medals from time to time, a different form of reward emerged and had the effect of eclipsing the development of decorations. This was the "*brevet commission*," or the conferring upon an officer a rank higher than that for which he was actually paid (until 1869, however, a brevet commission was fully valid for purposes of command and brevet holders received pay at their brevet ranks if they held a command appropriate to that rank). Although brevet commissions had been covered in the Articles of War, as adopted by the Congress, they first became emodied into law in section 4 of the Act of July 6, 1812, which provided that, "The President is hereby authorized to confer brevet rank on such officers of the army as shall distinguish themselves by gallant actions or meritorious conduct." This power was limited somewhat when, on April 6, 1818, the Congress enacted the proviso that, "...no brevet commission shall hereafter be conferred but by and with the advice and consent of the Senate." This restriction was apparently in response to abuses by the War Department which had manipulated commands and posts in order to match many brevet ranks with specific command positions so the holders of brevet commissions could receive pay commensurate with their brevet rank. Indeed, the brevet commission had been used to get around legal strength limitations during the Revolution and had thus been used for purposes other than rewarding valor or meritorious service.

Brevet promotions were widely used during the Civil War; however, four years after the war ended the law was again amended (on March 1, 1869) to provide that the brevet rank could not entitle its holder to "any increase in pay or emoluments." The Act further provided that all future brevet commissions would only be conferred in time of war and then only for "distinguished conduct and public service in presense of the enemy." This Act effectively killed the brevet promotion, for it also removed all privileges of command, except in the case of special assignment by the President. The final blow came in 1870 when Army regulations were revised to deny the holder of a brevet commission the right to wear the insignia of his brevet rank. The reasons for the 1869 Act are clear: during the latter part of the Civil War (and for several years thereafter) brevet commissions were issued in large numbers and with such a lack of discrimination that numerous scandals had arisen. A great many of the brevets were awarded to officers for "faithful and meritorious service" behind the desks of the War Department, and for service in other jobs which involved not only no actual conflict with the enemy but also not even most of the ordinary hardships or other dangers of war. At the time of the passage of the 1869 Act there were numerous brevet commissions before the Senate, although the war had been over for four years, and there was good reason to believe the flood of brevet nominations would continue for years to come unless stopped by some type of legislative action. The law of 1869 did stop the two prime abuses. First, it blocked the awarding of brevet commissions long after the renditon of the service for which it was to be conferred; and second, it blocked the conferring of brevet commissons in the future for non-combat service.

THE CERTIFICATE OF MERIT

America suffered one of her growing pains near the middle of the nineteenth century when she annexed Texas. The animosity between Mexico and the United States reached a breaking point, and on May 12, 1846, President Polk declared war on Mexico. The war called for courage and skill, and Congress was quick to see the need for prompt recognition of those qualities. On March 3, 1847, Congress enacted a law providing that "when any private soldier shall so distinguish himself" the President was authorized to grant him a Certificate of Merit. In 1854, noncommissioned officers were also made eligible for the award, which was to be granted specifically for "extraordinary exertion in the preservation of property, or rescuing from destruction by fire or otherwise, or any hazardous service by which the government is saved loss in men or materiel." Although the Certificate of Merit had no accompanying medal, its establishment was significant. In effect, it was the enlisted equivalent to the brevet commission. Second, it represented a "fixed" reward which remained constant in all cases, regardless of what the various winners had done to earn it. At a later date, it was also to provide the basis for the construction of a broad system of decorations for noncombat valor. The Certificate of Merit and the brevet commission stood side by side for seven years until the next step in the history of decorations was taken -- but that next step ultimately became the keystone of the entire system.

THE MEDAL OF HONOR

On December 21, 1861, Congress passed an Act to promote the efficiency of the Navy, and section 7 of that Act provided that, "The Secretary of the Navy be, and is hereby, authorized to cause two hundred medals of honor to be prepared with suitable emblematic devices which shall be bestowed upon such petty officers, seamen, landsmen and marines as shall most distinguish themselves by their gallantry in action and other seamanlike qualities during the present war...." The Bill was signed into law by President Abraham Lincoln and the first Federal decoration in the modern sense was thus brought into existence. It was followed nearly seven months later when, on July 12, 1862, Congress approved a Joint Resolution which provided for the establishment of a similar Medal of Honor for the Army. The Medal of Honor has become and remains the keystone of our system of military and naval decorations.

The development of military and naval decorations has been guided by three major trends. The first has been to distinguish between decorations awarded for valor and those which are given for outstanding achievement or meritorious service. Decorations for outstanding achievement recognize some notable act or specific accomplishment, while decorations for meritorious service typically reward the outstanding performance of normal duties over a period of time. Quite clearly, heroism is in a class by itself, and it has been necessary to establish decorations which distinguish between heroism and other forms of achievement or service. The military and naval decorations for heroism are open to all ranks and obviously represent the most prestigious awards. Not all decorations make this clear distinction, however. Some of them (such as the Bronze Star Medal or the Distinguished Flying Cross) can be awarded for either heroism or outstanding achievement.

The second major trend has been in developing distinctions among the degree of merit to be rewarded. This has been necessary in order to protect the "higher" decorations while at the same time ensuring that suitable decorations are available for individuals who perform noteworthy (but lesser) acts of heroism, outstanding achievement, or meritorious service. Thus we have, for example, decorations which reward achievement starting with the Achievement Medals and extending upward through the Commendation Medals, the Meritorious Service Medal, the Legion of Merit or Defense Superior Service Medal, and finally to the Distinguished Service Medals. A comparable chain exists for decorations for heroism. Although this system has become complex, it effectively rewards extraordinary performance - heroic or otherwise - at virtually all levels of the armed forces.

The third trend has been the development of decorations which are unique to the service branch making the award. There is a small core of decorations common to all service branches (the Silver Star, Legion of Merit, Distinguished Flying Cross, Bronze Star, Meritorious Service Medal, and Purple Heart); all others are unique to a particular service. Even though the decorations may be unique to a given service branch, there is a parallel structure among the service branches. For example, the Navy Cross is directly comparable to the Distinguished Service Cross (Army) and the Air Force Cross. The most recent trend has been the establishment of decorations unique to the Department of Defense; yet even these decorations parallel their service branch counterparts (thus the Defense Superior Service Medal is the Defense Department's equivalent to the Legion of Merit, and so on).

Military and naval decorations are generally similar in size and overall design. For example, most decorations are in a shape other than round (which is usually reserved for campaign or service medals), although there are exceptions. According to some observers, in recent years the careful artistic design of decorations and adherence to traditions of design have diminished and there has also been criticism over the large number of decorations. However, in spite of these issues it is clear that the United States does have a sophisticated if complex system of military and naval decorations.

I would like to express my gratitude to those who have helped in the preparation of this book. Special thanks goes to John E. Lelle who reviewed the manuscript and made many valuable suggestions. Without his generous help and encouragement, this book would never have become a reality. I would also like to thank Albert F. Gleim for his comments, in particular on the Certificate of Merit. Jeanne Kirke of the Department of the Navy made numerous important records available to me and likewise encouraged this undertaking. Dr. Oscar P. Fitzgerald of the Navy Memorial Museum proved to be a good colleague and ardent supporter, and I wish to thank him on behalf of the Museum and the Navy Historical Foundation for allowing me to use many of the medals in their collection to illustrate this book. Finally, unless otherwise indicated, the photos were taken by William Micick and to him must go all credit for their quality.

THE MEDAL OF HONOR

Gideon Welles, Secretary of the Navy from March 7, 1861 to March 3, 1869. Welles selected the design for the original Medal of Honor in 1862. (US Navy photo)

In 1861 Senator James Grimes of Iowa, Chairman of the Senate Naval Committee, took an interest in the subject of awards. As a result, he introduced a bill in Congress which was a landmark in the history of United States decorations. On December 21, 1861, Congress enacted this bill when it passed an "Act to Promote the Efficiency of the Navy." Section 7 of this Act provided that, "The Secretary of the Navy be, and is hereby, authorized to cause two hundred medals of honor to be prepared with suitable emblematic devices which shall be bestowed upon such petty officers, seamen, landsmen and marines as shall most distinguish themselves by their gallantry in action and other seamanlike qualities during the present war...."

The first federal decoration (in the modern sense) was created when Senator Grimes' bill was signed into law by President Abraham Lincoln. The exact wording of the Act is important, for it appears that the Congress actually intended for the Medal of Honor to be temporary (restricted to the Civil War), fixed in number (two hundred), and to be divided among those most qualified. Five months after the enactment authorizing the Medal of Honor, Secretary of the Navy Gideon Welles received a letter from James Pollock, who was at that time Director of the United States Mint. In his letter dated May 9, 1862, Pollock advised Welles that design number one, which had been submitted on May 6, 1862, by Christian Schussel, had been approved and would be adopted as the official design for the Navy's Medal of Honor. Pollock went on to describe the scene on the medal as one in which "The foul spirit of secession and rebellion is represented in a crouching attitude holding in his hands serpents, which with forked tongues are striking at a large figure representing the Union or Genius of our country, who holds in her right hand a shield and in her left the fasces. Around these figures are thirty-four stars, indicating the number of the states composing the Union. At the top of the medal or star is the holder, in the form of an anchor around which a cable is entwined indicating the naval service." This symbolism lends clear support to the thesis that the medal was specifically considered to be a Navy award for service during the Civil War.

However, three months after Welles wrote his letter to Pollock, Congress passed another act (on July 16, 1862) which provided that "Seamen distinguishing themselves in battle or by extraordinary heroism in the line of their profession may be promoted to forward warrant officers or acting master's mates, as they may best be qualified, upon the recommendation of the commanding officer, approved by the flag officer and the department. Upon such promotion they shall receive a gratuity of one hundred dollars and a medal of honor to be prepared by the Navy

Department." This second act raises several interesting questions. Did the "medal of honor" referred to in the second Act refer to the same "medal of honor" authorized by the Act of December 21, 1861 (which had been limited to two hundred)? Or, did it intend for a special medal to be designed for each recipient as had been done on several occasions in the past? Also, did the medal of honor created by the second act constitute a reward in and of itself, or was it intended to represent the brevet promotion for valor? What did the Navy intend to be more meaningful: the one hundred dollars, the promotion, or the medal? The facts of the case indicate that the Navy intended by the second act to issue the same medals of honor prepared under the aegis of the Act of December 21, 1861, if for no other reason than it was more economical and would save time. However, since the Act of July 16, 1862, did not restrict its provisions to the Civil War, it made (at least in theory) the Medal of Honor a permanent decoration. The fact that the medal itself was probably considered trivial is suggested by its being accompanied by one hundred dollars and a promotion. However, this should come as no surprise, for as of the passage of the Act of 1862 none of the medals had yet been awarded. The glory and esteem in which the Medal of Honor would subsequently be held had to wait for an accumulation of deeds yet to be performed.

On February 17, 1862, Senator Henry Wilson of Massachusetts introduced a Senate Resolution proposing a similar medal of honor for enlisted men of the Army. Accordingly, on July 12, 1862, Congress approved a Joint Resolution which provided that the "President of the United States be, and he is hereby, authorized to cause two thousand medals of honor to be prepared with suitable emblematic devices, and to direct that the same be presented in the name of Congress, to such noncommissioned officers and privates as shall most distinguish themselves by their gallantry in action, and other soldier-like qualities, during the present insurrection." This Joint Resolution was amended by Section 6 of the Sundry Civil Appropriations Act of March 3, 1863, to allow commissioned officers of the Army to receive the medal and to remove the "other soldier-like qualities" proviso. This left gallantry in action as the sole qualification for the Army Medal of Honor. The Act of July 12, 1862, restricted the total number of Army Medals of Honor to two thousand and specified that they were to be awarded for acts performed during the Civil War, implying that the Army Medal of Honor was to be a temporary decoration.

When he heard that a Medal of Honor was being considered for the Army, Secretary of the Navy Welles wrote to Secretary of War Edwin M. Stanton suggesting that the basic design adopted by the Navy might also be appropriate for the Army. Secretary Stanton agreed. Thus, with minor differences, the Army and Navy shared a medal of honor similar in design for a number of years.

The first Army Medals of Honor were presented on March 25, 1863, to six survivors of a group of twenty-two volunteers who were members of a raiding party sent to sabotage the vital rail link between Atlanta and Chattanooga in April of 1862. The first Navy Medals of Honor were awarded on April 3, 1863, to a number of sailors for various acts of gallantry during attacks on Forts Jackson, Fisher, and St. Philip a year earlier (April 24, 1862).

Both the design of the Medal of Honor and the laws which govern it have changed over the years. The best way to describe these changes is to break them down chronologically by service branch.

THE FIRST NAVY MEDAL OF HONOR: *December 21, 1861, to August 11, 1913.*

As already noted, the first style Medal of Honor was designed by Christian Schussel and the dies were made from a model prepared by Anthony Paquet. The Schussel design is a five-pointed star in bas relief with trefoils. In the center of each arm of the star is a crown of oak and laurel, combining the two ancient symbols for achievement and valor. Surrounding the center of the star, and forming a base to each of its arms, is an annulet charged with thirty-four stars representing the number of states in the Union as of 1861 (the United States government never recognized the Confederate states as having left the Union, and they are therefore represented among the thirty-four stars in the annulet). In the center of the medal is Columbia, previously described, who is warding off Discord. The star is suspended by an anchor which is connected to the medal itself by two suspension rings which pass through holes drilled in the star and then cross over the flukes of the anchor. The anchor is entwined (or *fouled*) in rope (or by a *line*, to use correct naval parlance) and hangs from a suspension ring which passes through the base of an open fasces which has a star in its center. The ribbon passes through a bar on the back of the fasces and then through a fasces of identical design (minus the star) at the top of the ribbon. This upper fasces is the pin bar by which the medal was to be affixed to the wearer's uniform. The ribbon itself was one inch wide and is a variation of the United States flag. At the top of the ribbon is a field of dark blue and the bottom is divided into alternating stripes of red (seven) and white (six). The reverse of the medal is blank; however, prior to its presentation it was to be inscribed with the words, *PERSONAL VALOR*, to be followed by the name of the recipient, his rank, ship, and the place and date of the deed for which the medal was awarded.

Navy Medal of Honor
(1862 - 1913)

THE SECOND NAVY MEDAL OF HONOR: *August 12, 1913, to April 5, 1917.*

The Navy's second style of Medal of Honor was a slight modification of the first. In order to standardize the ribbons of Medals of Honor earned by Army and Navy personnel, a joint board recommended that the ribbon to the Navy Medal of honor be changed from the flag design to the type then being used by the Army. As a result, on August 12, 1913, the Secretary of the Navy issued an order changing the ribbon to light blue silk charged with

Navy Medal of Honor
(1913 - 1917)

thirteen white stars. At the same time, the medal was simplified somewhat by removing the lines from the anchor which suspended the star. The new regulation specified that thereafter the medal was to be worn "on a cravat, pendant from the neck." However, one often sees Navy Medals of Honor of this vintage in which the blue ribbon has been threaded through the fasces used in the first syle Medal of Honor. Also, on March 3, 1915, the Medal of Honor was opened to commissioned ranks (up until this time, the Navy Medal of Honor could not be awarded to officers).

THE THIRD NAVY MEDAL OF HONOR: *April 6, 1917, to August 7, 1942.*

The third Navy Medal of Honor represented an entirely different design. On February 4, 1919, Congress authorized this Medal of Honor for award to any person in the naval service who while in action involving "actual conflict" with the enemy distinguished himself conspicuously by gallantry and intrepidity at the risk of his life above and beyond the call of duty. However, the old Medal of Honor was retained for award to those who distinguished themselves by extraordinary heroism in the line of their profession - but not in direct conflict with an armed enemy.

Navy Medal of Honor
(1917 - 1942)

This Medal of Honor was designed by Tiffany & Company of New York and is often referred to as the *Tiffany Cross.* It is a gold plated bronze cross patee, 35 millimeters across, on a wreath of oak and laurel leaves. The center of the cross bears the eagle design from the United States seal within an octagon bearing the inscription, *United States Navy, 1917-1918.* A plain anchor appears on each arm of the cross. The reverse is plain except for the words, *AWARDED TO.* The medal is suspended from a pale blue ribbon charged with thirteen white stars. The stars are arranged in a triple chevron pointing to the top of the ribbon. At the top of the ribbon is a gold plated bar which contains the word *VALOR.*

THE FOURTH NAVY MEDAL OF HONOR: *August 7, 1942, to the present.*

On August 7, 1942, Congress readopted the Schussel five-pointed star, to be suspended by an anchor from a neckband of pale blue under a pad (also pale blue) charged with thirteen white stars. There have been some minor modifications of the neck ribbon and the pad with the stars, but the medal as adopted by the Act of August 7, 1942, is basically the same medal awarded to Navy and Marine Corps personnel today.

Navy Medal of Honor
(1942 - present)

FOR DISTINGUISHED
CONDUCT IN THE
PRESENCE OF THE
ENEMY, IN BATTLES
ON THE 13TH, 20TH, 21ST,
AND 22D OF JUNE, 1900, WHILE
WITH THE RELIEF EXPEDITION
UNDER VICE ADMIRAL SEYMOUR
TO
FRANK GALLAGHER, B.M.1/C

reverse

In implementing the legislation authorizing the original Medal of Honor the Navy issued General Order Number 10, dated April 3, 1863, which provided that anyone who, after having received the Medal of Honor, again performed an act which would justify an additional award of the medal, would be granted the authority to wear a bar attached to the ribbon and that, for each additional act of the kind, an additional bar would be so added. In spite of the fact that several people did earn more than one Medal of Honor, there is no record of any such bar having been designed, procured, or presented.

In order to protect the reputation of its Medal of Honor, the Navy enacted a regulation which provided that "...if any person on whom it shall have been conferred be subsequently convicted of treason, cowardice, felony, or any infamous crime; or if he be accused of any such offense and does not, after a reasonable time, surrender himself to be tried therefore, his name shall forthwith be erased from the registry ... by a General Order from the Secretary of the Navy, who alone is to be the judge of the circumstances demanding the expulsion."

By the Acts of March 3, 1901, and of March 3, 1915, the award of a Medal of Honor was authorized to any officer or enlisted man of the Navy or Marine Corps "who shall have distinguished himself in battle or displayed extraordinary heroism in the line of his profession." The Act of February 4, 1919, while not repealing the earlier laws, authorized the presentation of a Medal of Honor to any person who, while in the naval service, shall "...in action involving actual conflict with the enemy, distinguish himself conspicuously by gallantry and intrepidity at the risk of his life above and beyond the call of duty...." Following the Act of 1919 Medals of Honor continued to be awarded (under the authority of the earlier Acts) for deeds of extraordinary heroism in the line of one's profession. However, in accordance with Bureau of Navigation *Circular Letter No. 36-27* of 19 March 1927, the Navy adopted the policy that the award of a Navy Medal of Honor would only be recommended for cases involving gallantry and intrepidity in action against an armed enemy, as per the act of February 4, 1919. In spite of this official policy, the Navy Medal of Honor continued to be awarded for non-combat heroism until the practice was barred by Public Law 702 of August 7, 1942.

THE FIRST ARMY MEDAL OF HONOR: *July 12, 1862, to May 1, 1896.*

The first Army Medal of Honor incorporated the same five-pointed star in bas relief by Schussel that the Navy used. It also employed the same kind of ribbon. The only differences between the first Army and Navy Medals of Honor were the pin clasp used to attach the medal to the uniform and the device from which the star was suspended from the ribbon. The Army medal was suspended from its ribbon by a trophy composed of crossed cannons above eight stacked cannon balls and a sabre; at the top of the trophy is an eagle behind whose extended wings there runs a bar through which the ribbon is looped. The cannon, shot, and sabre represent the artillery and cavalry, the prime combat forces of the time. The eagle is of course the national symbol. The top of the ribbon looped through a pin bar composed of a shield (taken from the Great Seal of the United States) between two cornucopia which symbolize America as the land of plenty.

Army Medal of Honor
(1862 - 1896)

The medal, suspension device, and pin were made of gun metal and are dark brown in color. As in the case of the Navy Medal of Honor, the reverse was left blank so it could be engraved with the recipient's name, rank, company, regiment, and the place and date of the action for which the medal was to be awarded. Whereas the Navy Medals of Honor were engraved with the words, *PERSONAL VALOR* the Army medals were engraved with *THE CONGRESS TO.*

THE SECOND ARMY MEDAL OF HONOR: *May 2, 1896, to April 23, 1904.*

Many of the veterans of the Civil War were active in a number of veteran's organizations and other patriotic societies. These organizations frequently gave their members badges which were at best thinly disguised replicas of the Medal of Honor. To deal

Army Medal of Honor
(1896 - 1904)

with this problem, Congress passed a Joint Resolution on May 2, 1896, authorizing the President to prescribe and establish a new ribbon for the Army Medal of Honor and authorizing the Secretary of War to issue the new ribbon to those who held a Medal of Honor - providing the earlier ribbon "shall have been lost, destroyed, or rendered unfit for use, without fault or neglect on the part of the person to whom it was issued...." To implement this Joint Resolution, on November 10, 1896, the Secretary of War issued an order providing that the ribbon was to be "...of silk one inch wide and one inch in length; the center stripe of white one-sixteenth of an inch wide, flanked on either side by a stripe of blue seven thirty-seconds of an inch wide, bordered by two stripes of red each one-quarter of an inch wide." The basic colors of the original ribbon were not changed - their positions were simply altered.

THE THIRD ARMY MEDAL OF HONOR: *April 23, 1904, to 1944.*

Army Medal of Honor
(1904 - 1944)

In spite of the change to its ribbon, the Army Medal of Honor continued to be widely copied. Late in 1903, Brigadier General Horace Porter had several designs prepared by Messrs Arthur, Bertrand, & Berenger of Paris. He sent the designs to the Army's Adjutant General and recommended that one of them be selected as a revised design for the Army's Medal of Honor. The designs were given to the Medal of Honor Legion, and following approval by that organization the Secretary of War granted his approval for the design they had selected. Representative Cordell Hull of Tennessee introduced a Bill in 1904 which would authorize the new medal, which was passed on April 23, 1904.

To fully protect this new design, a patent was sought. On November 22, 1904, General George L. Gillespie was granted Patent Serial Number 197,369 covering the new Medal of Honor. General Gillespie then assigned the patent for the new Medal of Honor to "W.H. Taft and his successor or successors as Secretary of War of the United States of America." The new Medal of Honor was officially described as being made of silver, heavily electroplated in gold. The shape retained the basic Schussel design of a five-pointed star with trefoils. The medal is one and nine-sixteenths of an inch in circumscribing diameter, and its center contains a bust of Minerva, the symbol for wisdom and righteous war, in profile facing to the viewer's right. In an annulet surrounding the figure of Minerva are the words, *UNITED STATES OF AMERICA* and at the base of the annulet is a small shield, taken from the Great Seal of the United States. The star is superimposed over an open laurel wreath, which runs between the arms of the star. The laurel wreath, as well as the crowns of oak within each arm of the star, are enameled in green to give them prominence. The star is suspended by a bar containing the word *VALOR* and over which is an eagle with its wings extended and its talons bearing arrows and a branch of olive. The medal is suspended by a blue silk ribbon spangled with thirteen white stars, representing the original states. Although the ribbon had a pin-back, the medal could be affixed to a pale blue neck ribbon and worn pendant about the neck.

The exact reason for the selection of the color and shade of blue which was adopted is open to question. The color blue is symbolic of loyalty and vigilance and was probably suggested by the color of the union of the United States flag or because dark blue has been officially recognized as the national color since 1821. The particular shade of blue may have been derived from the light blue ribbon sash which General George Washington prescribed for wear by the Commander-in-Chief. Perhaps the light shade of blue was adopted simply because it gave a suitable contrast to the dark blue uniforms worn by the Army at the turn of the century.

THE FOURTH ARMY MEDAL OF HONOR: *1944 to the present.*

The fourth Army Medal of Honor - the one which is currently awarded - is simply the third type with a new neck ribbon. The neck ribbon is the same shade of blue but contains a pad from which the medal is suspended. The pad is also pale blue and contains the thirteen white stars. This ribbon and the size of the pad have been modified slightly over the years but the design has remained essentially the same since it was adopted.

Army Medal of Honor
(1944 - present)

In its early years, the Medal of Honor was the only decoration the Army had. It became obvious over the years that in some cases it had been awarded for acts for which it was clearly inappropriate. In order to strengthen the integrity of the medal, Section 122 of the National Defense Act of June 3, 1916, provided for the establishment of an Army board of review which was to examine all awards of the Medal of Honor and to eliminate those which were deemed inappropriate. By October 16, 1916, the board had met and began to gather data and study individual cases. Between October 16, 1916, and January 17, 1917, all of the 2,625 Medals of Honor which had been awarded as of that date were reviewed. On February 15, 1917, nine hundred and eleven names were stricken from the list. Those removed included the 864 medals awarded to the members of the 27th Maine Volunteers, six that went to similar regiments, the 29 Medals of Honor that were awarded to the honor guard that accompanied Lincoln's body home after he was assassinated, five medals that went to Indian Scouts (including the one awarded to Buffalo Bill Cody), and seven which were miscellaneous awards not earned in combat. As an interesting historical footnote, one of the seven miscellaneous Medals of Honor was awarded to Dr. Mary Walker, a contract surgeon of bizzare character who had served with the Army during the Civil War. As a result of intensive lobbying by feminists Dr. Walker's Medal of Honor was restored by the Carter administration.

THE US AIR FORCE MEDAL OF HONOR: *November 1, 1965, to the present.*

After becoming a separate service in 1947, the U.S. Air Force continued to award medals and decorations of the Army design. However, the Air Force later decided that it would be more appropriate to award medals of its own design and accordingly secured legislation permitting it to do so. Air Force decorations are generally considered as deriving from their earlier comparable Army awards; that is, they are not legally "new" decorations but rather the Air Force design versions of previously established Army decorations. The Air Force is authorized to issue its own version of the Army Medal of Honor by Section 8741 of Title 10 of the U.S. Code. The Air Force Medal of Honor became effective on November 1, 1965, and was designed by Lewis J. King, Jr., of the Army's Institute of Heraldry. The version selected was the fifth design submitted. The medal is officially described as follows: within a wreath of laurel in green enamel, a gold finished five-pointed star, one point down, tipped with trefoils and each point containing a crown of laurel and oak on a green enamel background. Centered upon the star is an annulet of thirty-four stars which surround the profile of the head from the Statue of Liberty.

The star is suspended by a connecting bar and pinned hinge from a trophy consisting of a bar inscribed with the word *VALOR* above an adaptation of a thunderbolt. The bar is suspended from a pale blue moire silk neckband behind an elongated square pad in the center, with the corners turned back and charged with thirteen white stars in the form of a triple chevron. The star is a replica of the design originally adopted by the Navy and the Army. The profile taken from the Statue of Liberty represents those ideals for which the United States is known throughout the world. The thunderbolt is taken from the Air Force coat of arms and distinguishes the medal as an Air Force decoration. The medal is two inches in overall height and two and one-sixteenth inches in overall width, making it larger than either the Army or Navy Medals of Honor. The reverse is plain, providing space for the name of the recipient.

The first Air Force Medal of Honor was presented by President Lyndon B. Johnson on January 19, 1967, to Major Bernard F. Fisher, a soft-spoken Mormon fighter pilot who earned his medal during a daring and courageous combat rescue of a downed pilot in Vietnam.

Air Force Medal of Honor

The Medal of Honor is currently awarded under three circumstances: (1) while engaged in action against an enemy of the United States, (2) while engaged in military operations involving conflict with an opposing foreign force, or (3) while serving with friendly foreign forces engaged in an armed conflict against an opposing armed force in which the United States is not a belligerent party. The last provision was enacted to allow the Medal of Honor to be awarded during periods of undeclared war (as in Vietnam).

For award of the Medal of Honor there must be no margin of doubt or any possibility of error: to justify the Medal of Honor, an individual must clearly render himself conspicuously above his comrades by an act so outstanding that it clearly distinguishes his gallantry as being beyond the call of duty. It must be the type of deed which if not done would not leave him open to criticsm, and must be done without detriment to his mission or to the command to which he is attached. Further, the recommendation must be submitted within three years of the act, and the medal must be awarded within five years of the act (there have, however, been exceptions to the rules governing the timing of recommendations and awarding the Medal of Honor). The Medal of Honor is the highest decoration which can be awarded to a member of the armed forces, making it the most prestigious decoration the United States can grant -- and the most difficult to earn.

Medals of Honor awarded to Commander Richard E. Byrd, Jr. (left) and Machinist Floyd Bennett, USN. Both received the Medal of Honor for sevice "between the wars." Bennett received his medal for "courage and intrepidity at the risk of his life as a member of the Byrd Arctic Expedition and thus contributing largely to the success of the first heavier-than-air flight to the North Pole and return." Byrd won his for "distinguishing himself conspicuously by courage and intrepidity at the risk of his life, in demonstrating that it is possible for aircraft to travel in continuous flight from a now inhabited portion of the earth over the North Pole and return." Note the type of medal each received: the "Tiffany Cross" which was intended for combat valor during the First World War.

THE MARINE CORPS BREVET MEDAL

(Obsolete)

On April 16, 1814, Congress authorized the President to "*confer brevet rank on such officers of the Marine Corps as shall distinguish themselves by gallant actions or meritorious conduct, or who shall have served ten years in any one grade.*" The practice of granting "brevet" promotions was widely employed in both the Army and the Marine Corps during the nineteenth century. A brevet promotion was an advancement in rank (normally without an increase in pay or other benefits) as a reward for heroic or meritorious service.

Although brevet promotions were popular during the nineteenth century, they also proved to be the source of several problems. The practice was subject to abuse, and in addition it created large numbers of officers in the higher ranks. The establishment of decorations eclipsed the practice of awarding brevet promotions, and they gradually fell into disuse.

However, in the early years of this century there were still a number of officers on active duty who held brevet promotions. These individuals were members of a small group of heroes whom Major General John Archer Lejeune, the thirteenth Commandant of the Marine Corps (July 1, 1920 to March 4, 1929), wished to publicly recognize. In a letter dated April 12, 1921, General Lejeune recommended to the Secretary of the Navy that an appropriate medal, badge or ribbon be prescribed as an article of uniform to denote that the wearer had received a brevet promotion, issued by the President and confirmed by Congress. Lejeune pointed out that the legality of the use of certain available funds for this purpose had been established by the Comptroller General in a decision on the subject dated December 18, 1907. In his endorsement of May 13, 1921, the Secretary of the Navy authorized the Commandant to submit the design of an appropriate medal, and on June 7, 1921, the medal was officially approved. The Brevet Medal was specifically authorized for issue to any officer holding a brevet commission for "distinguished conduct and public service in the presence of the enemy" during the Mexican War, the Civil War, the Spanish-American War, the Philippine Insurrection, or the Boxer Rebellion. The medal was not to be awarded posthumously, thus assuring that it would be given to only a limited number of recipients. Because of this restriction, the USMC Brevet Medal was rendered obsolete the day it was issued.

obverse

reverse

Brevet Medal

The Brevet Medal was designed by Quartermaster Sergeant Joseph A. Burnett, who worked under the supervision of Brigadier General Charles L. McCawley (a recipient of the Brevet Medal), who was Quartermaster General of the Marine Corps. The medal is a bronze cross pattee, with each arm extended in a semi-circular shape; in the center of the cross is the word *BREVET* encircled by the words, *UNITED STATES MARINE CORPS.* A small Marine Corps insignia (globe, anchor, and eagle) is used to attach the medal to its suspension ring. The reverse of the medal is plain except for the legend, *FOR DISTINGUISHED SERVICE IN THE PRESENCE OF ENEMY.* The medal is suspended by a ribbon of scarlet moire spangled with thirteen white stars. The USMC Brevet Medal was designated as second in precedence only to the Medal of Honor.

Recipients of the USMC Brevet Medal

BANNON, Philip M. Breveted to first lieutenant on June 13, 1898, for "*distinguished service in battle at Guantanamo, Cuba.*"

BUTLER, Smedley D. Breveted to captain on July 13, 1900, for "*distinguished conduct and public service in the presence of the enemy near Tientsin, China, July 13, 1900.*"

GAMBORG-ANDRESEN, Carl Breveted to Captain on July 13, 1900, for "*distinguished conduct and public service in the presence of the enemy near Tientsin, China.*"

HALL, Newt H. Breveted to major on August 14, 1900, for "*distinguished conduct in the presence of the enemy at the siege of Peking, China.*"

KELTON, Allan C. Breveted to major on July 3, 1898, for "*distinguished conduct and public service in the presence of the enemy at Guantanamo, Cuba.*"

LONG, Charles G. Breveted to captain on June 11, 1898, for "*distinguished conduct and public service in the presence of the enemy at Guantanamo, Cuba.*"

LUCAS, Lewis C. Breveted to captain on June 13, 1898, for "*conspicuous conduct in battle at Guantanamo, Cuba.*"

MAHONEY, James E. Breveted to captain on June 11, 1898, for "*distinguished conduct and public service in the presence of the enemy at Guantanamo, Cuba.*"

McCAWLEY, Charles L. Breveted to major on June 11, 1898, for "*distinguished conduct and public service in the presence of the enemy at Guantanamo, Cuba.*"

Brigadier General Charles L. McCawley, USMC (1929). General McCawley, as Quartermaster General of the Marine Corps, urged Major General John A. Lejeune to push for establishment of the Brevet Medal. McCawley received the Brevet Medal for service during the Spanish-American War. (USMC photo)

McKELVEY, William N., Sr. Breveted to captain on June 11, 1898, for "*distinguished conduct and public service in the presence of the enemy at Guantanmo, Cuba.*"

MURPHEY, Paul St. Clair Breveted to major on July 3, 1898, for "*gallant service in the naval battle of Santiago, Cuba.*"

MYERS, John T. Breveted to major on July 20, 1900, for "*distinguished conduct in the presence of the enemy at the defense of the legations at Peking, China.*"

NEVILLE, Wendell C. Breveted to captain on June 13, 1898, for "*conspicuous conduct in battle at Guantanamo, Cuba.*"

POPE, Percival C. Breveted to captain on September 8, 1863, for "*gallant and meritorious service in the night attack upon Ft. Sumter.*"

PORTER, David D. Breveted to captain on October 8, 1899, for "*distinguished conduct and public service in the presence of the enemy at Novaleta, Philippine Islands.*"

POWELL, William G. Breveted to captain on June 21, 1900, for "*distinguished conduct and public service in the presence of the enemy at Tientsin, China.*"

RICHARDS, George Breveted to lieutenant colonel on July 13, 1900, for "*distinguished conduct in the presence of the enemy at the battle of Tientsin, China.*"

SHAW, Melville J. Breveted to first lieutenant on June 11, 1898, for "*distinguished conduct and public service in the presence of the enemy at Guantanamo, Cuba.*"

THORPE, George C. Breveted to captain on October 8, 1899, for "*distinguished conduct and public service in the presence of the enemy at Novaleta, Philippine Islands.*"

WALLER, Littleton W.T. Breveted to lieutenant colonel on July 13, 1900, for "*distinguished conduct and public service in the presence of the enemy near Tientsin, China.*"

Three officers were scheduled to receive the Brevet Medal, however they died before it was ready. Since the Brevet Medal was not to be presented posthumously, the next of kin of these officers did not receive the medal. They were James Forney (breveted three times - twice during the Civil War and once for service in Formosa in 1867), Louis J. Magill (breveted during the Spanish-American War), and, Albert S. McLemore (breveted during the Spanish-American War).

Sgt Joseph A. Burnett, USMC (1925). As a Quartermaster Sergeant in 1921, Burnett designed the USMC Brevet Medal under the direction of Brigadier General Charles L. McCawley. (Courtesy USMC).

IN REPLYING
REFER TO No.

HEADQUARTERS U. S. MARINE CORPS.

01204-3
AG-1-1tr

WASHINGTON. November 16, 1921.

From: The Major General Commandant.
To: Brigadier General Percival C. Pope, Marine Corps, Retired, 59 Morton Road, Milton, Mass.

Subject: Brevet medal.

Reference: (a) Marine Corps Order No. 26, (1921).

Enclosures: (2) Brevet medal; receipt card.

1. The undersigned takes pleasure in transmitting to you with this letter, the Brevet medal which is awarded in accordance with reference (a) for the following citation:

"POPE, PERCIVAL CLARENCE

On March 2, 1867, appointed Captain, by brevet, to rank from September 8, 1863, for gallant and meritorious service in the night attack upon Fort Sumter."

John A Lejeune

obverse

reverse

Certificate of Merit Medal

THE CERTIFICATE OF MERIT

(Obsolete)

During the Mexican War (1846-1847) the Army saw the need to recognize and reward enlisted soldiers who distinguished themselves in action. However, at the time of the Mexican War the United States did not have medals or decorations as we know them. Therefore, there was no existing method of recognizing gallantry in action on the part of the common "private" soldier.

As a result, Congress passed the Act of March 3, 1847, providing that "the President be empowered to grant a certificate of merit to any private soldier who has distinguished himself by gallantry performed in the presence of the enemy." The act also provided that any private soldier who received such a certificate of merit would also receive an additional two dollars pay per month so long as he was a private and remained on continuous active duty. Noncommissioned officers who distinguished themselves by gallantry in action were to be rewarded by a brevet promotion to second lieutenant.

A total of 539 Certificates of Merit were awarded to privates for gallantry in action during the Mexican War. The first Certificate of Merit was awarded to Pvt. John R. Scott, Company B, 2nd Dragoons, for heroism at the Battle of Cerro Gordo, Mexico, on April 17, 1847. There were no Certificates of Merit awarded for service during the Civil War, primarily because the War Department took the position that the Act of March 3, 1847, (which established the Certificate of Merit) was only intended to recognize gallantry during the Mexican War. In addition, during the Civil War the Army received authority to award the Medal of Honor, and acts which would have previously earned a Certificate of Merit were certainly those for which the Medal of Honor was appropriate.

After the Civil War many recommendations for award of a Certificate of Merit were submitted to the War Department. These were routinely turned down because the War Department continued to take the position that the legislation creating the Certificate of Merit limited its award to the Mexican War. However, as a result of intensive lobbying by some senior Army officers, the Certificate of Merit was restored in 1877 by Secretary of War George W. McCrary who held that the Certificate of Merit could be awarded under the provisions of existing federal law. June 22, 1874, was established as the earliest date for which recommendations would be accepted for new awards.

Clarification of the requirements for a Certificate of Merit were issued in Article XXVI of Army Regulations for 1889, which provided that the Certificate of Merit was to be awarded for extraordinary acts of gallantry by private soldiers in the presence of the enemy, that the recommendation had to originate with an eyewitness (preferably the private's commanding officer), and that the extra pay was to commence as of the date of the action for which the certificate was awarded.

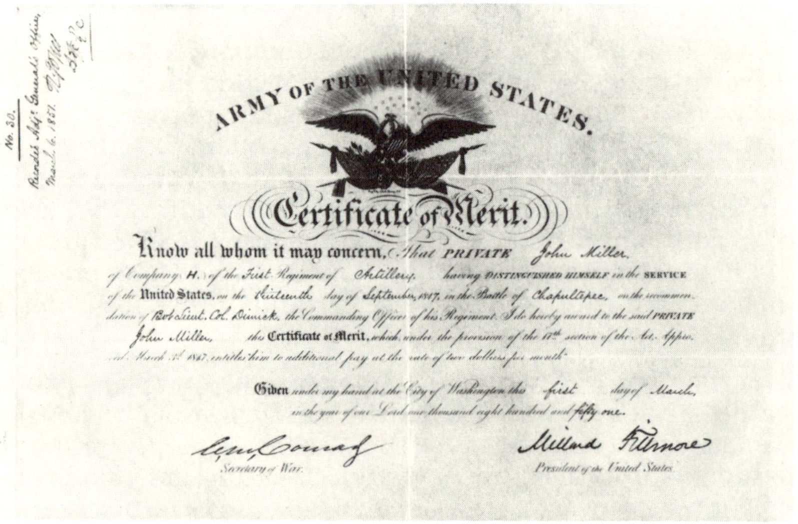
ARMY OF THE UNITED STATES.

Certificate of Merit.

Know all whom it may concern, That PRIVATE John Miller of Company H. of the First Regiment of Artillery having DISTINGUISHED HIMSELF in the SERVICE of the United States, on the thirteenth day of September, 1847, in the Battle of Chapultepec, on the recommendation of Bvt. Lieut. Col. Dimick, the Commanding Officer of his Regiment, I do hereby award to the said PRIVATE John Miller, this Certificate of Merit, which, under the provision of the 17th section of the Act approved March 3d 1847, entitles him to additional pay at the rate of two dollars per month.

Given under my hand at the City of Washington this first day of March, in the year of our Lord one thousand eight hundred and fifty one.

Geo. W. Conrad, Secretary of War.

Millard Fillmore, President of the United States.

Certificate of Merit to Private John Miller of Company H, First Regiment of Artillery, for distinguished conduct on September 13, 1847, at the Battle of Chapultepec during the war with Mexico.

A significant amendment to the rules governing award of the Certificate of Merit came about through an Act of Congress of February 3, 1891, which provided that the Certificate of Merit could also be awarded for specially meritorious service in time of peace and further authorized award of the Certificate to noncommissioned officers. The fact that the Certificate of Merit could now be awarded for non-combat service required additional clarification as to the kinds of acts for which it would be appropriate. This was forthcoming when Major General John M. Schofield defined the distinction between the Medal of Honor and the Certificate of Merit in a circular published by the Adjutant General on March 29, 1892, which stated that: "Medals of Honor should be awarded to officers or enlisted men for distinguished bravery in action, while Certificates of Merit should, under the law, be awarded for distinguished service whether in action or otherwise, of valuable character to the United States, as, for example, extraordinary exertion in the preservation of human life, or in the preservation of public property, or rescuing public property from destruction by fire or otherwise, or any hazardous service by which the government is saved loss in men and materiel. Simple heroism in battle, on the contrary, is fitly rewarded by a Medal of Honor, although such an act of heroism may not have resulted in any benefit to the United States."

Public Law 193 of July 9, 1918, establishing the Distinguished Service Medal and the Distinguished Service Cross also provided that "...said distinguished service medal shall be issued to all enlisted men of the Army to whom the certificate of merit has been granted up to and including the date of the passage of this Act, under the provisions of previously existing law, in lieu of such certificate of merit, and after the passage of this Act the award of the certificate of merit for distinguished service shall cease; and additional pay heretofore authorized by law for holders of the certificate of merit shall not be paid to them beyond the date of the award of the distinguished service medal in lieu thereof as aforesaid." The law went on, however, to state that "...each enlisted man of the Army to whom there has been or shall be awarded ... a distinguished-service medal shall, for each such award, be entitled to additional pay at the rate of two dollars per month from the date of the distinguished act or service on which the award is based...." Thus, after 71 years and 4 months America's oldest active decoration ceased to exist.

The Distinguished Service Medal was established to recognize outstanding performance in a duty of great responsibility. Since most Certificates of Merit were awarded for heroism, it was decided that an award of the Distinguished Service Cross in lieu of the Certificate of Merit would be more appropriate. Accordingly, Public Law 114 of March 5, 1934, provided that "...the Distinguished Service Cross shall be issued to all enlisted men of the Army to whom the Certificate of Merit was issued under the provisions of previously existing law in lieu of such Certificate of Merit." The law also required those who had previously received a Distinguished Service Medal in lieu of an earlier award of a Certificate of Merit to surrender the Distinguished Service Medal to the War Department in order to receive the Distinguished Service Cross.

During its lifetime a total of 1,206 Certificates of Merit were awarded. Their distribution was as follows:

Mexican War	539
Indian Wars	61
Spanish-American War	203
Philippine Insurrection	175
Boxer Rebellion	21
Mexican Border (1915-1916)	2
Lifesaving	133
Saving Government Property	23
Accidents or Natural Disasters	23
Law Enforcement	16
Health Services	10

On January 11, 1905, War Department General Order Number 4 authorized the creation of a medal to accompany the Cerificate of Merit. The medal was designed by Francis D. Millet, and is a circular bronze medallion in the center of which is an eagle with wings partially spread, facing the viewer's left, surrounded by the Latin inscription, *VIRTUTIS ET AUDACIAE MONUMENTUM ET PRAEMIUM* (courage and virtue are their own monument and reward). On the reverse of the medal, in the center, are the words *FOR MERIT* encircled by a wreath composed of oak, joined at the base by a bow. The wreath is, in turn, encircled by an annulet composed of the words *UNITED STATES ARMY* in the upper half, and thirteen stars in the lower half. The ribbon is composed of two bands of red, white, and blue with the blue on the outside and the red stripes separated by a narrow stripe of white. These represent the National colors.

The symbolism of the medal is quite interesting. Millet selected this particular eagle "...from the most perfect representation of a Roman war eagle in existence, the life-sized marble antique in the possession of Lord Weyms, formerly Lord Elcho, well known for his great interest in the British volunteers." The eagle is intended to be symbolic of both the Roman war eagle and the American bald eagle. The Latin inscription was selected, according to Millet, because it "was used in the time of the revolution" and because "the word *MERIT* on the obverse of the medal seemed to me to be altogether commonplace, and this opinion is shared, I may say, by everyone to whom I have spoken about it." On the reverse, the oak is the traditional symbol of strength and courage, and the thirteen stars represent the thirteen original states.

The Certificate of Merit medals were serially numbered on the lower rim, and a record of each medal was maintained by the Adjutant General's office. A total of 354 Certificate of Merit medals were issued between December 30, 1907 and June 21, 1919. Of the 354 persons who received the Certificate of Merit Medal, 270 subsequently applied for and received a Distinguished Service Medal. A total of 75 recipients of the Certificate of Merit Medal applied for and received the Distinguished Service Cross (including 57 who had previously applied for and received the Distinguished Service Medal).

Distinguished Service Cross
(First Style)

Distinguished Service Cross
(Current style)

DISTINGUISHED SERVICE CROSS

(U.S. Army)

On July 5, 1911, Major General Leonard Wood, the Army's Chief of Staff, advised Secretary of War Henry L. Stimson that a need existed for a decoration of lesser importance than the Medal of Honor, and suggested the establishment of a "distinguished-service medal" which could be awarded to both officers and enlisted men. The proposal met with very little support until the outbreak of the First World War when the Army found itself in the embarassing position of still not having an appropriate decoration for distinguished non-combat service or for heroism not justifying a Medal of Honor. Moreover, the Army had no decoration which could be awarded to foreign military personnel, nor did it have a decoration which a field commander could present to a deserving soldier within a relatively short period of time after the "heat of battle." This last point was important, as many heroes were so badly wounded that they either died of their wounds or had to be evacuated quickly. Army authorities wanted a decoration similar to Great Britain's Military Cross (founded on December 31, 1914) or France's Croix de Guerre (established on April 8, 1915).

The issue of military decorations had also developed into something of a political issue after America entered the war. One reason was that American soldiers could not wear foreign decorations. In fact, on November 26, 1917, the *New York Times* reported that fifteen American soldiers -- the first to withstand an enemy attack since the United States entered the war -- had been awarded the French Croix de Guerre but had to put them in their pockets because regulations forbade them from wearing them.

The restriction against U.S. troops accepting and wearing allied decorations was soon set aside, and in November of 1917 General John J. Pershing, commander of the Allied Expeditionary Force, recommended that authority be granted to award some sort of medal for meritorious or distinguished service. On December 28, 1917, the Secretary of War responded by officially recommending to President Woodrow Wilson that a Distinguished Service Cross and a Distinguished Service Medal be authorized. Accordingly, on January 9, 1918, President Wilson authorized the two decorations. This was followed three days later (on January 12, 1918) by the promulgation of War Department General Order Number 6 (which was republished as General Orders Number 26, GHQ, American Expeditionary Forces, on February 11, 1918) which authorized the two decorations as official U.S. Army awards. Congress confirmed the two decorations in its appropriations act for the support of the

Army for the fiscal year ending June 30, 1919 (the act was approved on July 9, 1918). This particular piece of legislation provided, in part, that "...the President be ... authorized to present, but not in the name of Congress, a distinguished service cross ... to any person who, while serving in any capacity with the Army of the United States since the sixth day of April, nineteen hundred and seventeen, has distinguished or who shall hereafter distinguish himself in connection with military operations against an armed enemy.

After the Distinguished Service Cross was authorized, the Army solicited designs for the medal. The approved design was submitted by Captains Andre Smith and Aymar E. Embury, based on sketches drawn by Col. J.R.M. Taylor. A model of the cross was sculpted by Private Gaetano Cecere (who, along with Smith and Embury, was assigned to Company B, 40th Engineers - Camouflage Section - at Camp American University in Washington, D.C.). The first samples of the new Distinguished Service Cross were placed on public exhibition in Washington in April of 1918.

The original design of the Distinguished Service Cross met with some heated criticism from the National Sculpture Society. Mr. Paul W. Bartlett, president of the society, not only criticized the design of the cross, but was also displeased "...as the medals were being made by a Philadelphia firm of silversmiths." The firm to which Bartlett referred was Bailey, Banks and Biddle, a noted Philadelphia jewelry company (Bartlett was wrong: the Distinguished Service Crosses were struck at the Philadelphia Mint).

Bartlett sent a formal protest to Secretary of War Newton D. Baker on June 14, 1918, in which he alleged that the medal was of an inferior artistic design. Baker forwarded Bartlett's protest to President Wilson for his comments, and on June 17, 1918, received the following reply:

> My Dear Baker,
>
> What do you think yourself about the advisability of having these medals artistically reconsidered by the official art commission? They are fine in a way, but they are merely the designs of a jeweler's house and lack the delicacy of workmanship which I should like to see them exhibit, and yet I don't want to have the matter gone over again if you think it would be unwise to do so.
>
> Cordially and sincerely yours,
>
> (signed, Woodrow Wilson)

Secretary Baker responded on June 25, 1918, with the following letter:

My Dear Mr. President:

I enclose a sample of the Distinguished Service Cross. It and the Distinguished Service Medal were designed by Captain Aymar Embury, who is an architect of most delightful personality and, so far as I have been able to judge, or to learn, of distinguished artistic taste and ability. He came to Washington at the outbreak of the war in the interest of a camouflage section and was one of the leaders in the group of fine young men, including St. Gaudens and others, whom you met at the American University at the camouflage exhibition.

The dies for these medals have already been cast and the medals are being made, and I question the wisdom of reopening this particular case. It would perhaps have been well if the Department had referred Captain Embury's designs to the National Sculpture Society through the Fine Arts Commission, and as a matter of fact, the Society has since been informed that future work of this kind will be so referred.

I do not know enough to have an independent judgment about the artistic value of this Cross; but General March and others here in the Department insist that field-won decorations like this from the military point of view should have no intrinsic value. The Iron Cross given by the German Emperor is actually of iron, and each is worth about two cents.

The intention with regard to the Distinguished Service Cross and Medal is ultimately to have them made of captured German war materials, and as they will doubtless be conferred in very great numbers it is suggested by General March that anything which adds greatly to their cost or slowness of manufacture would be unfortunate.

To my mind, this Cross is good. Its simplicity and freedom from too great embellishment appeal to me strongly. Admittedly, finer detail work might be done upon it, but when one considers the nature of the decoration I doubt whether greater refinement would be appropriate. A substantial number of these decorations have already been sent to General Pershing; but of course they could be exchanged for any later medal deemed better.

I frankly do not think it will be possible to get any medal which will satisfy the artists of the country, and my disposition would be to let the matter rest where it is with the Cross and the Medal as already designed; but I am too conscious of my own infirmity of judgment about an artistic matter to be all sure that I am right.

May I have back the sample Cross herewith enclosed, with any expression of your judgment in the matter which you are willing to give me for my guidance?

Respectfully yours,

(signed, Newton D. Baker)

President Wilson agreed with Baker, as he expressed in his letter to him on June 26, 1918:

My Dear Baker:

Thank you for having let me see the enclosed sample cross for distinguished service. I wish the original design had been submitted to the Art Commission, but I dare say you are right in thinking that it would not be well to begin over again now, and I must say that the cross itself seems to me dignified and interesting enough.

Cordially and faithfully yours,

(signed, Woodrow Wilson)

Even before President Wilson's decision to let the matter of the design of the Distinguished Service Cross rest, action had been initiated to change its design. On April 11, 1918, the Acting Quartermaster General sent a letter to the Adjutant General which stated in part that "...upon examining the first of the crosses and medals struck at the Mint, it was considered advisable to make certain minor changes that would add to the beauty and attractiveness of the same, which are now being carried into effect...." The letter went on to say that, "Appreciating the importance of hastening the supply of the crosses and Medals of Honor, for which cable requests have been received from General Pershing commanding the American Expeditionary Forces in France, 100 crosses, numbered 1 to 100 have been struck off from the original die ... for transmission to General Pershing and are ready for shipment at the Philadelphia Depot."

The Adjutant General acknowledged the letter on April 15, 1918, and stated that, "...a careful record will be kept of the persons to whom the crosses in question will be issued in order that the crosses may be replaced at some later date." The Distinguished Service Crosses of the first design were thus sent to France by a special courier and were awarded by General Pershing.

First style Distinguished Service Cross. Dissatisfaction with the design led the President of the National Sculpture Society to complain to the Secretary of War, who in turn passed the criticism on to President Wilson. The design was modified, and only 100 of the original crosses were struck. (Photo by James W. Schaaf)

Reverse of the first style Distinguished Service Cross. (Photo by James W. Schaaf)

Close-up photo of first style Distinguished Service Cross showing how the medal was numbered. (Photo by James W. Schaaf)

The first Distinguished Service Cross awarded went to First Lieutenant John N. Greene of Staunton, Virginia. Greene had gone to France in January of 1917 and had served six months with a field ambulance service. In September of 1917 he was commissioned a second lieutenant in the field artillery and after six days training was sent to the front. In December of 1917 he was one of forty-seven men General Pershing recommended for promotion and was subsequently promoted to first lieutenant. On March 1, 1918, while he was on duty in a dugout near Toul, France, he was painfully wounded in the leg by a grenade fragment. An attacking party of Germans ordered him to surrender, but Greene killed one with his pistol and drove the others away. In addition to receiving the Distinguished Service Cross for this act, Greene was also given the Croix de Guerre by the French government.

The first style Distinguished Service Cross is a modified bronze crosslet 45.9 mm wide and 53 mm high. On the obverse, in each arm of the cross, are oak leaves; in the center of the cross is a four-pointed diamond with one point centered in each arm of the cross. At each point of the diamond is a five-pointed star. Superimposed within the diamond is an eagle with its wings spread, extending into the upper re-entrant angles of the cross. A scroll (taken from the obverse of the Great Seal of the United States) appears beneath the eagle and extends through the lower re-entrant angles and runs behind the lowest point of the diamond. Within the scroll is the inscription, *E PLURIBUS UNUM* ("from many, one" which refers to the fact that the United States is one nation composed of many states). The reverse of the medal is plain except for a plaque bearing the inscription, *FOR VALOR*. The plaque is enclosed within a wreath of laurel and is superimposed over a decorative mace.

The revised (current) version of the Distinguished Service Cross is very similar in design to the original version. It is 49.2 mm high and 42.2 mm wide. The oak leaves have been removed and the eagle is superimposed over a laurel wreath instead of the diamond. The scroll is pierced and contains the inscription, *FOR VALOR*. The reverse still has the plaque, but it is blank (for engraving the recipient's name). The ribbon is moired silk and has a central field of blue edged in white and red.

In terms of symbolism, the eagle reresents the bald eagle and symbolizes the United States; the oak leaves on the first style cross stand for strength and the laurel wreath (on the reverse of the first style but on the obverse of the second style) represent victory. The colors of the ribbon are those of the flag and stand for purity (white), sacrifice (red), and high purpose (blue).

Close-up view of the numbering on Edgar A. Jennings' Distinguished Service Cross.

The first style Distinguished Service Crosses were numbered from one 1 to 100; the second style Distinguished Service Crosses were numbered from 1 to an unknown number. An effort was made to record the names and numbers of all recipients; however, the practice was not carried forward into World War II and Distinguished Service Crosses numbered above 8000 cannot be traced.

Although the law which created the Distinguished Service Cross specifically stated that it was to be awarded for acts performed on or after April 6, 1917, there are a number of instances in which it was awarded for acts performed much earlier. Some of these awards represent conversions from the Certificate of Merit; however, several are "original" awards. The reason for this is quite interesting.

After the turn of the century, a number of nominations for brevet promotions were forwarded to the Senate for confirmation. However, these recommendations were never acted upon because the Senate took the position that the law governing the award of brevet promotions required that the nominations be sent to the Senate while the war was still in progress. In this case, the wars involved (the Spanish-American War, the Philippine Insurrection, and the Boxer Rebellion) had been successfully concluded. Therefore, the recommendations for brevet commissions for extraordinary heroism in action produced no results. To correct this inequity, the House Committee on Military Affairs favorably reported H.R. 2192 authorizing the award of the Distinguished Service Cross to officers who had been nominated by the President for brevet promotions for extraordinary heroism during the Spanish-American War, the Philippine Insurrection, or the Boxer Rebellion. As a result, 131 Distinguished Service Crosses were awarded for services rendered prior to the First World War:

Indian Wars	6
Spanish-American War	30
Philippine Insurrection	60
Boxer Rebellion	6
Mexican Border Service	5
Miscellaneous Service	24

The Distinguished Service Cross is currently awarded to a person who, while serving in any capacity with the Army, distinguishes himself by extraordinary heroism not justifying the award of a Medal of Honor while (a) engaged in an action against an enemy of the United States, (b) while engaged in military operations involving conflict with an opposing foreign force, or (c) while serving with friendly foreign forces engaged in an armed conflict in which the United States is not a belligerent party. The act or acts of heroism must have been so notable and have involved risk of life so extraordinary as to set the individual apart from his comrades.

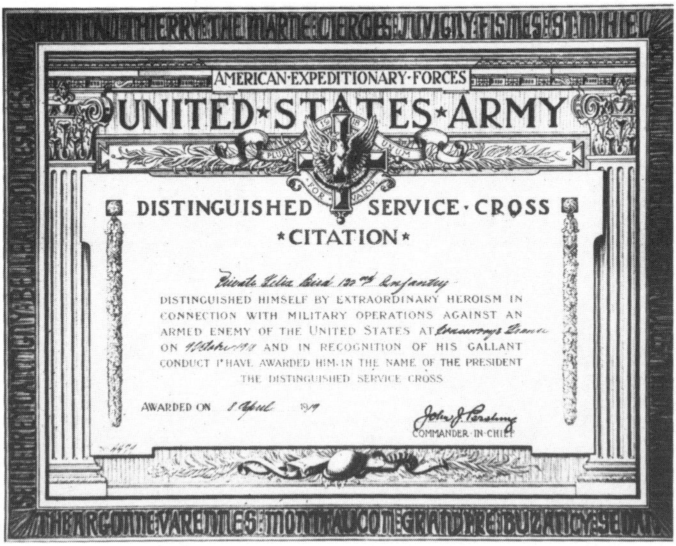

AMERICAN·EXPEDITIONARY·FORCES

UNITED★STATES★ARMY

DISTINGUISHED SERVICE·CROSS

★CITATION★

Private Felix Bird [illegible] Infantry

DISTINGUISHED HIMSELF BY EXTRAORDINARY HEROISM IN CONNECTION WITH MILITARY OPERATIONS AGAINST AN ARMED ENEMY OF THE UNITED STATES AT [illegible] France ON [illegible] AND IN RECOGNITION OF HIS GALLANT CONDUCT I HAVE AWARDED HIM IN THE NAME OF THE PRESIDENT THE DISTINGUISHED SERVICE CROSS

AWARDED ON 8 April 1919

John J. Pershing
COMMANDER-IN-CHIEF

Original Distinguished Service Cross certificate, signed by General Pershing.

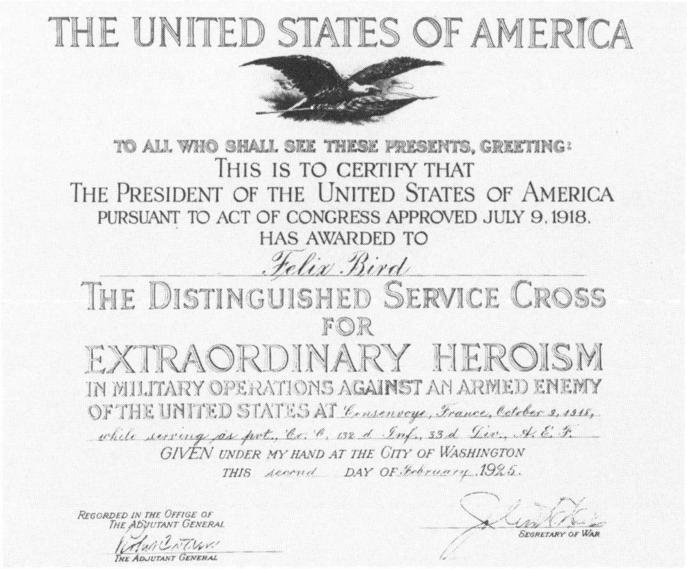

THE UNITED STATES OF AMERICA

TO ALL WHO SHALL SEE THESE PRESENTS, GREETING:
THIS IS TO CERTIFY THAT
THE PRESIDENT OF THE UNITED STATES OF AMERICA
PURSUANT TO ACT OF CONGRESS APPROVED JULY 9, 1918,
HAS AWARDED TO
Felix Bird
THE DISTINGUISHED SERVICE CROSS
FOR
EXTRAORDINARY HEROISM
IN MILITARY OPERATIONS AGAINST AN ARMED ENEMY
OF THE UNITED STATES AT Consenvoye, France, October 9, 1918,
while serving as pvt., Co. C, 132 d Inf., 33 d Div., A. E. F.
GIVEN UNDER MY HAND AT THE CITY OF WASHINGTON
THIS second DAY OF February 1925.

RECORDED IN THE OFFICE OF
THE ADJUTANT GENERAL

THE ADJUTANT GENERAL

SECRETARY OF WAR

Later (1925) Distinguished Service Cross certificate issued by the War Department.

obverse

reverse

Navy Cross

THE NAVY CROSS

At the outbreak of the First World War the Navy faced the same problem that had confronted the Army: it did not have a decoration below the Medal of Honor which it could award for acts involving a lesser degree of valor. The Army had solved this same problem through the passage of Public Law 193 by the 65th Congress, which established the Distinguished Service Cross.

Following the Army's lead, the Navy sought the creation of decorations for heroism and distinguished service, and as a result the Navy Cross and the Navy Distinguished Service Medal were established by Public Law 253 by the 65th Congress. This Act, which was passed on February 4, 1919, provided that "...the President be ... authorized to present, but not in the name of Congress, a Navy Cross of appropriate design ... to any person who, while in the naval service of the United States, since the sixth day of April, nineteen hundred and seventeen, has distinguished, or shall hereafter distinguish, himself by extraordinary heroism or distinguished service in the line of his profession, such heroism or service not being sufficient to justify a Medal of Honor or a Distinguished Service Medal."

Two problems soon emerged. The first involved the matter of precedence. The wording of the law meant that the Navy Cross could be awarded for acts performed in either combat or peacetime and that it was inferior in rank to the Distinguished Service Medal (which had been created by the same Act) -- even though the Navy Distinguished Service Medal was intended to be awarded only for non-combat acts. The second problem stemmed from the fact that the Navy Cross was actually established after the First World War had been over for three months.

Even though the war was over, Secretary of the Navy Josephus Daniels wanted to award appropriate decorations to members of the naval service for acts rendered during the war. Accordingly, on March 6, 1919, he appointed a board to be headed by Rear Admiral (Retired) Austin M. Knight "...for the purpose of recommending to the Department those persons who are, in accordance with the terms of the act of Congress approved February 4, 1919, deemed by the board worthy of the award of medals of honor, distinguished service medals, and Navy crosses provided for in said act."

Instructions were sent out in early 1919 requesting interested parties to submit recommendations to the Board. Unfortunately, those who were asked to make recommendations were not given any consistent guidelines for making their recommendations. The Knight Board began considering recommendations on March 17, 1919, and continued in session until October 31, 1919, when it was

Secretary of the Navy (1913-1921) Josephus Daniels. A strong-willed and energetic man, Daniels was a major figure in the early awards of Navy decorations -- which brought him into conflict with senior Naval officers. (US Navy photo)

dissolved by Secretary Daniels, even though its work was not yet completed. The Knight Board had scrutinized over 4000 recommendations and had submitted three reports to the Secretary. Each report contained the Board's recommendation for decoration(s) to be awarded to each individual.

Secretary Daniels considered the Knight Board to be advisory only and reserved the right to make all final award decisions. He finally published an awards list as a part of his annual report for the year 1919. When the list was released it produced considerable unhappiness among many senior officers. Only 41.5 percent of the Secretary's awards matched the recommendations of the Knight Board (or of the commanding officers who had originally made

Rear Admiral Austin M. Knight (from a pre-World War I photo). Knight was chairman of the board appointed by Secretary of the Navy Daniels to consider recommendations for Navy decorations for service during the First World War. (US Navy photo)

their recommendations to the board). More specifically, 18.5 percent of thc awards wcrc rcduccd from what had been originally recommended, 2 percent were upgraded, and 38 percent were awards made by the Secretary without any previous recommendation by either commanding officers in the field or the Knight Board.

The uproar was so great that Daniels reconvened the Knight Board on December 26, 1919, and informed them that "...no official approval of any list has been made. All lists published were tentative." The numerous complaints that had been made, however, resulted in the establishment of a subcommittee of the Congressional Committee on Naval Affairs to investigate "awarding of medals in the Naval service." Hearings opened on January 16, 1920, and concluded on February 10, 1920. The report of the subcommittee was published on March 7, 1920, and was critical of Secretary Daniels on several points. For example, the Secretary awarded at least 30 Distinguished Service Medals for heroism although such acts should have been rewarded with a Navy Cross. He was also criticised for giving duplicate awards to Marine Corps personnel who had been previously awarded Army decorations (for example, Marines who won a Distinguished Service Cross were also given a Navy Cross). This resulted in the awarding of 4 Medals of Honor, 12 distinguished Service Medals, and 309 Navy Crosses to individuals who had already received comparable Army decorations.

The Knight Board completed its second review of recommendations after a session which lasted from January through June of 1920. However, Secretary Daniels again took the position that the board's recommendations were only advisory and again issued his own list of awards. His second list, which was issued on Armistice Day of 1920, differed in many respects from what the Knight Board had recommended.

Thus, the Navy Cross was not only established too late to be awarded during the war, it was surrounded by controversy and in some cases, bitterness. Because some Navy Distinguished Service Medals had been awarded for heroism, the Navy Cross was viewed by some as inferior -- especially since it had been awarded for such things as "distinguished service in the line of his profession while serving on the staff of the commander of the United States Naval forces operating in European waters," or for "exceptionally meritorious service in a duty of great responsibility as head of department of seamanship, U.S. Naval Academy...." The Navy Cross lacked a clear identification as a decoration for heroism and its position was somewhat ambiguous.

This was changed during World War II with the passage of Public Law 702 on August 7, 1942. This Act elevated the Navy Cross above the Navy Distinguished Service Medal and restricted it to acts performed in the presence of an armed enemy, placing it on a par with the Army's Distinguished Service Cross. Thus by passage of this Act, the Navy Cross become second only to the Medal of Honor and its prestigeous order of precedence was clearly established

The Navy Cross was designed by James Earle Fraser. It is a modified cross patee (the ends of its arms are rounded whereas a conventional cross patee has arms that are straight on the end) and is one and one half inches wide. It has four laurel leaves with berries in each re-entrant angle, symbolic of victory. In the center of the obverse is a sailing vessel on waves (sailing to the viewer's left). The vessel is characteristic of a type in use during the period of about 1480 to 1500 (referred to at the time as a "caravel") and represents the tradition of the sea. In the center of the reverse are crossed anchors of the pre-1850 period, with cables attached. the letters USN appear amid the anchors. The ribbon is of the standard dimensions (one and three-eighths inches wide) and is navy blue moired silk with a center stripe of white.

The Navy Cross was not numbered nor has it usually been engraved with the recipient's name. According to current regulations, the Navy Cross is awarded to any person who, while serving with the Navy or Marine Corps, distinguishes himself by extraordinary heroism not justifying the awarding of a Medal of Honor. The action must take place (1) while engaged in action against an enemy of the United States, (2) while engaged in military operations involving conflict with an opposing foreign force, or (3) while serving with friendly foreign forces engaged in an armed conflict in which the United States is not a belligerent party.

To earn a Navy Cross, the act to be commended must be performed in the presence of great danger or at great personal risk and must be performed in such a manner as to render the individual highly conspicuous among others of equal grade, rate, experience, or position of responsibility. An accumulation of minor acts of heroism does not justify an award of the Navy Cross. During its entire history, only about 7000 Navy Crosses have been awarded.

obverse

reverse

Air Force Cross

THE AIR FORCE CROSS

The United States Air Force was created by the National Security Act of 1947 and began operating as a separate service on September 18, 1947. The USAF descended from several predecessor organizations, starting with the Aeronautical Division of the Army Signal Corps in 1907 and going through the Army Air Force, which was established during World War II. When the USAF was created, the same law which brought it into existence transferred the personnel and facilities of the old Army Air Force over to the new USAF.

The Air Force also carried over all of the decorations authorized for the Army and continued to award them under Air Force authority. However, by the 1950's interest had developed in establishing a set of decorations with designs unique to the Air Force. A staff study done in 1956 recommended the creation of certain Air Force decorations, and over the next three years additional studies on the subject supported the suggestion.

A key feature of the proposed "new" Air Force decorations is that they are not authorized as totally new decorations, but rather as redesigned and renamed versions of their Army predecessors. Thus, the Air Force Cross is a derivative of the Distinguished Service Cross, as can be clearly seen in its design and ribbon. Public Law 86-593 (which came into effect on July 6, 1960) amended Section 8742 of Title 10, United States Code, to change the designation "Distinguished Service Cross" to "Air Force Cross" in the case of awards made under Air Force Authority. The Air Force Cross is, therefore, the Air Force version of the Distinguished Service Cross.

The Air Force Cross is given for extraordinary heroism, not justifying the award of a Medal of Honor, to any person, who while serving in any capacity with the U.S. Air Force (a) while engaged in an action against an enemy of the United States, (b) while engaged in military operations involving conflict with an opposing foreign force, or (c) while serving with friendly foreign forces engaged in an armed conflict against an opposing armed force in which the United States is not a belligerent party. Like the Distinguished Service Cross, the Air Force Cross is presented in the name of the President, although the Air Force itself actually controls its award.

The original design of the Air Force Cross was made by Eleanor Cox, an employee of the Air Force, and her design was sculpted by Thomas Hudson Jones of the Army's Institute of Heraldry. It is described as a bronze cross with an oxidized satin finish. Centered on the cross is a gold-plated American bald eagle, wings displayed against a cloud formation, encircled by a laurel wreath finished in green enamel. The design is conceptually and symbolically very close to the Distinguished Service Cross. The scroll on the Distinguished Service Cross (which contains the words *FOR VALOR*) has been removed, and the cloud formation behind the eagle (taken from the Air Force crest) has been added. The laurel wreath is much more prominent on the Air Force Cross than it is on the Distinguished Service Cross and is highlighted with green enamel. The reverse of the Air Force Cross is blank, leaving room for engraving the recipient's name. The ribbon for the Air Force Cross is identical to that of the Distinguished Service Cross, except that the blue used in the center stripe is the lighter shade of Brittany Blue.

To date, fewer than two hundred Air Force Crosses have been awarded. The first Air Force Cross went to Major Rudolf Anderson, Jr., who was killed in action on October 27, 1962 when, his U-2 surveillance plane was shot down by a surface-to-air missile over Cuba during the Cuban Missile Crisis. The Air Force Cross was then going into production and no finished examples were available for award. However, one was specially assembled for presentation by General Thomas S. Power (who was then the commander in chief of the Strategic Air Command) to Major Anderson's widow.

Although Anderson received the first Air Force Cross, his act was not the earliest to be so rewarded. In 1943, Second Lieutenant William J. Sloan of the 96th Fighter Squadron was recommended for a Distinguished Service Cross for shooting down two German aircraft in a single day. Although his recommendation was approved, the paperwork got lost and the Distinguished Service Cross was never presented. Long after World War II was over, Sloan's son pursued the matter of the lost Distinguished Service Cross. In 1969 Sloan, then a retired lieutenant colonel, received an Air Force Cross based on his heroism twenty-six years earlier!

Sloan is not the only World War II winner of the Air Force Cross. In May of 1983, Secretary of the Air Force Vernon Orr presented the Air Force Cross to Urban L. Drew, a fighter ace who had earned the decoration on October 7, 1944 when he attacked and shot down two German Me-262 jets near Hamm, Germany. Although Drew, like Sloan, was recommended for the Distinguished Service Cross for this action, the recommendation never reached higher headquarters. In 1983 a review by the Air Force Board for the Correction of Military Records resulted in a determination that Drew should receive the Air Force Cross, which was accordinly awarded by the Secretary of the Air Force.

Although the majority of the awards of the Air Force Cross have been for extraordinary heroism in action while engaged in aerial flight, there is no requirement that the action involve flight. Several have been awarded for extraordinary heroism while a prisoner of war; one was awarded posthumously to Captain Reginald V. Maisey, Jr., (one of two Security police officers to win the Air Force Cross) for his heroic defense of the perimeter of Bien Hoa Air Base on January 31, 1968. Other Air Force Crosses have been awarded for ground action (primarily during search and rescue operations). In one instance the Air Force Cross was awarded for the handling of an aircraft emergency. In 1975 a C-5 aircraft suffered catastrophic failure of the elevator flight controls while climbing out from Ton Son Nhut Air Base, Republic of Vietnam. On board was a plane load of Vietnamese orphans. For his handling of the emergency crash landing which resulted, Captain Dennis W. Traynor was awarded the Air Force Cross -- the only such award for a non-combat aerial mission (the reason Traynor's act qualified for the Air Force Cross was because the incident took place in what was technically a combat zone).

Major Rudolph Anderson, Jr. Major Anderson was a U-2 pilot who lost his life during the Cuban missile crisis when he was shot down on October 27, 1962, by an antiaircraft missile. He received the first award of the Air Force Cross, which was presented posthumously to his widow. (USAF photo)

obverse

reverse

Defense Distinguished Service Medal

THE DEFENSE DISTINGUISHED SERVICE MEDAL

Numerous senior officers have held assignments which have placed them in a position of authority over elements of other service branches. In fact, the so-called unified or "joint commands," consisting of elements of all service branches, are the standard organizations through which most major military operations are conducted. In the past it has been accepted practice for one service branch to award its own Distinguished Service Medal to senior officers of other service branches when their leadership in a joint command justified the award. For example, General Dwight D. Eisenhower, who was the Supreme Commander, Allied Forces Europe, received not only the Army's Distinguished Service Medal but the Navy's as well.

It has also become customary for the acting or former Chairmen of the Joint Chiefs of Staff to be awarded the individual Distinguished Service Medals of each of the services upon retirement. For example, on September 1, 1969, General Lyman Lemnitzer received the Army, Navy, and Air Force Distinguished Service Medals at the ceremony marking his retirement from his position as Supreme Allied Commander, Europe. However, Secretary of Defense Melvin Laird was reported to have remarked that the use of the multiple decorations seemed improper and that a single decoration should be created for persons who serve in duties of unusual responsibility. Thus the idea of a "senior" Distinguished Service Medal was born.

The task of developing this new decoration was given to the Assistant Secretary of Defense for Manpower and Reserve Affairs, and by January of 1970 the project was well under way. In February of 1970, Secretary Laird further affirmed his desire to award a "Joint Distinguished Service Medal" and sought advice concerning the best way to authorize such a decoration. On March 26, 1970, the Office of the Assistant Secretary of Defense for Manpower and Reserve Affairs called the Army's Institute of Heraldry and told them that Secretary Laird wanted the medal designed, developed, and ready for presentation by July 3, 1970. In this initial contact with the Institute of Heraldry it was suggested that some elements from the seal of the Secretary of Defense be incorporated into the design of the medal.

Also on March 26, 1970, the Department of Defense General Counsel forwarded a memorandum for record to the Secretary of Defense (Director of Personnel and Management) discussing possible sources of authority for award of the proposed decoration. The memorandum noted that authority could be sought under an Act of Congress, an Executive Order, or through a

Department of Defense regulation. It was noted that a statute had the disadvantage of being difficult to enact and slow to obtain, but had the advantage of consistency with the source of authority for the Distinguished Service Medals of the other services.

An Executive Order was seen as having the disadvantage of possibly subjecting the President to criticism for creating a Distinguished Service Medal by executive fiat when the separate service medals were created by legislation. However, an Executive Order had the advantage of being more easily promulgated than a statute and had the prestige of coming from the President. Finally, a Department of Defense regulation was seen as being the easiest way to get the decoration authorized, but was also the least prestigious. The General Counsel recommended that authority be sought under an Executive Order, even though such a move would produce a new precedent: it would create a decoration that ranked above several highly regarded, long-standing decorations which had been established by Act of Congress.

General Lyman L. Lemnitzer. General Lemnitzer's receipt of the Distinguished Service Medals of the Army, Navy, and Air Force in 1969 prompted Secretary of Defense Melvin R. Laird to recommend a single decoration be created to reward high ranking individuals who perform duties of unusual responsibility, leading to the establishment of the Defense Distinguished Service Medal. (US Army photo)

On March 27, 1970, an official memorandum from the Deputy Assistant Secretary of Defense (Military Personnel Policy) specifically stated that the Secretary of Defense had directed the medal be created and that it rank as the highest award for meritorious service within the Department of Defense. At the same time, the Institute of Heraldry was formally tasked to design and procure the medal no later than June 15, 1970. A proposed Executive Order establishing the medal was sent to the Bureau of the Budget on April 14, 1970. The next day, April 15, 1970, the Commission on Fine Arts approved the design proposed by the Institute of Heraldry. The proposed Executive Order was accepted, and E0 11545 (establishing the Defense Distinguished Service Medal) was signed by President Richard M. Nixon on July 9, 1970. The first Defense Distinguished Service Medal was awarded to General Earle G. Wheeler upon his retirement as Chairman of the Joint Chiefs of Staff.

First award of the Defense Distinguished Service Medal. Chairman of the Joint Chiefs of Staff, General Earle G. Wheeler, receives the Defense Distinguished Service Medal from Secretary of Defense Melvin R. Laird. The ceremony took place in a hangar at Andrews AFB, Maryland. (USAF photo)

The Defense Distinguished Service Medal was designed by Mildred Orloff and sculpted by Lewis J. King, Jr., both of the Army's Institute of Heraldry. The medal itself is gold in color and is one and seven-eighths inches in overall height. It features a medium-blue enameled pentagon (point up) superimposed by a gold eagle with outspread wings. The eagle's breast is charged with the shield of the United States, and the eagle is grasping three crossed arrows in its talons. The pentagon and eagle are enclosed within a gold, pierced circle consisting in the upper half of thirteen stars and in the lower half of a wreath of laurel on the left and olive on the right. At the top of the medal is a suspender composed of five graduated gold rays which extend above the stars. On the reverse of the medal, in relief, are the words, *FROM THE SECRETARY OF DEFENSE TO* and, *FOR DISTINGUISHED SERVICE.* The ribbon is composed of a central stripe of red flanked on either side by stripes of gold and blue.

The Defense Distinguished Service Medal is rich in symbolism: the eagle grasping the arrows is taken from the seal of the Secretary of Defense and is the American bald eagle. The pentagon in the background alludes to the Pentagon Building in Washington, D.C., which in turn represents the military services as well as the Office of the Secretary of Defense (all of which are headquartered in the Pentagon). The thirteen stars represent the thirteen colonies, and through them, all of the states. The olive branch represents the goal of defense - peace - while the laurel branch represents achievement.

Ironically, the separate service branches continue to award their respective Distinguished Service Medals to certain senior military and naval officers of other services -- even though the Defense Distinguished Service Medal was brought into existence to eliminate that practice!

One of the unique features of the Defense Distinguished Service Medal is that it is awarded by the Secretary of Defense and has no delegated authority; that is, the separate services cannot award the medal in the Secretary's name. It is not within the authority of the separate services to even initiate a recommendation for an award of the Defense Distinguished Service Medal or to provide supporting comments in favor of such a recommendation. The Defense Distinguished Service Medal is awarded solely at the initiative and pleasure of the Secretary of Defense.

Defense Distinguished Service Medal

The Defense Distinguished Service Medal is awarded by the Secretary of Defense to any military service officer, who while assigned to joint staffs and other joint activities of the Department of Defense, distinguishes himself by exceptionally meritorious service to the government in a position of unique and great responsibility. The Defense Distinguished Service Medal takes precedence over the Distinguished Service Medals of the separate services and is not to be awarded to any individual for a period of service for which an Army, Navy, Air Force or Coast Guard Distinguished Service Medal (or other decoration) is awarded.

obverse

reverse

Army Distinguished Service Medal

THE DISTINGUISHED SERVICE MEDAL

(United States Army)

On July 5, 1911, Major General Leonard Wood, Chief of Staff of the Army, submitted a report to Secretary of War Henry L. Stimson in which he noted that the need existed for a "suitable badge" to recognize distinguished service not of such a character as to be "of the most distinguished personal bravery or self sacrifice above and beyond the call of duty" for which the Medal of Honor was the appropriate reward. General Wood was of the opinion that the establishment of such a "badge" was especially important in the case of officers, as "...enlisted men may secure a Certificate of Merit for distinguished service, though the officer who participates with such enlisted men in this distinguished service must receive a Medal of Honor or nothing...."

General Wood (who won the Medal of Honor in 1886 during the campaign against the Apache Indians) felt that the lack of a lesser decoration had on occasion led to the awarding of the Medal of Honor to officers whose services were not sufficiently distinguished to have really justified the award, but who did deserve some kind of recognition. He felt that by adopting a "Distinguished Service Medal" as a reward for distinguished service other than in operations against an enemy, the cheapening of the Medal of Honor could be avoided. He also believed that the establishment of a Distinguished Service Medal would give the Army greater flexibility in rewarding heroism and distinguished service on the part of both officers and enlisted men. General Wood informed Secretary of War Stimson that "It would seem to lie entirely within the power of the President to divide ... distinguished service ... into two general classes: distinguished war service and distinguished peace service." This was the beginning of a concept that was ultimately to lead to the establishment of the Distinguished Service Cross and the Distinguished Service Medal.

The Secretary of War was interested in the proposal and referred General Wood's memorandum to the Judge Advocate General for his opinion. The Judge Advocate General studied the matter, and on September 9, 1911, sent the following reply:

> The question of the authority of the President to authorize medals was discussed by this office, and it was held that the power to award medals for distinguished service, or for any other purpose, rested in Congress, being, in its essentials, a legislative rather than an executive power. This view was accepted, and, as a result, when the campaign badges and the badge indicating a Certificate of Merit, were established the word ***badge,*** and the authority to issue such badges was based on the right of the President

> to prescribe the uniform of the Army. The opinion of this office was based, apparently, on the fact up to that date Congress alone had authorized medals to be issued for one purpose or another, and so far as the precedents are concerned, has established the right to provide this method of indicating achievement.

In spite of the somewhat negative attitude expressed by the Judge Advocate General's office, Secretary of War Stimson decided to press forward with the issue and asked the Quartermaster General to come up with a design for a distinguished service medal. On August 7, 1912, the Quartermaster's department filed a memorandum which took due note of the fact that the proposed distinguished service medal was to be given for "...service less conspicuous than those for which the Medal of Honor is given." This observation was followed by a recommendation that the Distinguished Service Medal be of a shape other than round and that the ribbon be red, as "...it is in keeping with the custom that the ribbon of the distinguished service medal, which will be the second prize for special services in the field be red in color, as the red ribbon is usually associated with the second prize." No further progress was made for the next six years.

After the United States entered the First World War, it became clear that the Army needed a decoration which rewarded outstanding performance in a duty of great responsibility. As a result, General Pershing asked the War Department to establish a Distinguished Service Medal for this purpose (this was part of the same request in which he also requested the establishment of a Distinguished Service Cross). Secretary of War Newton D. Baker passed General Pershing's request on to President Woodrow Wilson along with his recommendation that it be approved. On January 25, 1918, President Wilson authorized both medals. Both medals were subsequently confirmed by Congress on July 9, 1918.

On October 21, 1918, the first Distinguished Service Medals were awarded. They went to Marshall Foch (France), who was Commander in Chief of the Allied armies; Marshall Joffre (France), the victor of the first battle of the Marne; Field Marshall Sir Douglas Haig (England), Commander in Chief of British armies; General Petain (France), Commander in Chief of the French armies; Lieutenant General Diaz (Italy), Commander in Chief of the Italian armies; Lieutenant General Gillain (Belgium), Chief of Staff of the Belgian Army; and General John Joseph Pershing, Commanding General, American Expeditionary Forces.

The Distinguished Service Medal is awarded to any person who, while serving in any capacity with the United States Army, has distinguished himself by exceptionally meritorious service in a duty of great responsibility. The performance must be such as to merit recognition for service which is clearly exceptional. The exceptional performance of normal duties will not alone justify an award of the Distinguished Service Medal. The medal itself was designed by Captain Aymar Embury and sculpted by Gaetano Cecere. The obverse of the medal consists of the coat of arms of the United States in bronze surrounded by a circle of dark blue enamel one and one half inches in diameter bearing the inscription, *FOR DISTINGUISHED SERVICE* MCMXVIII. On the reverse there is a blank scroll upon a trophy of flags and weapons. The medal is suspended by a bar from a moired silk ribbon edged on both sides with a band of scarlet, a narrow band of dark blue, and a center band of white. The Distinguished Service Medal was originally numbered on the rim and a record maintained of each medal. However, this practice was discontinued during World War II and has not been revived.

As an interesting footnote, General Wood was awarded Distinguished Service Medal number 181 in 1919 for a variety of services he performed during the First World War.

General John J. Pershing. As Commander of the American Expeditionary Force he requested the establishment of the Distinguished Service Cross and Distinguished Service Medal (from a pre-World War I studio photograph).

obverse

reverse

Navy Distinguished Service Medal

THE DISTINGUISHED SERVICE MEDAL

(United States Navy)

At the time the United States entered the First World War the Navy did not have a decoration which could be awarded for distinguished service. Although the Navy did have the Medal of Honor, it could only be awarded for heroism and could not be given for other kinds of distinguished service. This problem was solved on February 4, 1919, with the passage of Public Law 253 (65th Congress), section two of which provided that, "The President be ... authorized to present, but not in the name of Congress, a distinguished service medal of appropriate design ... to any person who, while in the naval service of the United States since the sixth day of April, nineteen hundred and seventeen, has distinguished, or who hereafter shall distinguish, himself by exceptionally meritorious service to the Government in a duty of great responsibility."

Although section two of the law clearly indicated that the Navy Distinguished Service Medal was to be awarded for exceptionally meritorious service in a duty of great responsibility, section three of the same law provided that the Navy Cross was to be awarded for "extraordinary heroism or distinuished service in the line of his profession, such heroism or service not being sufficient to justify the award of a medal of honor or a distinguished service medal." In all probability, the intention of the law was to restrict the award of the Distinguished Service Medal to those who performed an outstanding service in a duty of great responsibility and to award the Navy Cross for either heroism (but not of a magnitude sufficient to deserve a Medal of Honor) or for distinguished service (but not of an order sufficient to warrant an award of the Distinguished Service Medal). The actual wording of the law was ambiguous and allowed for yet another interpretation: that the Distinguished Service Medal could be awarded for heroism greater than that which would justify the award of a Navy Cross, but not of a magnitude that would justify an award of the Medal of Honor. This ambiguity was to ultimately cause considerable unhappiness and embarrassment.

As has already been noted in the chapter dealing with the Navy Cross, Secretary Daniels convened a board under the chairmanship of Rear Admiral (retired) Austin M. Knight to receive and evaluate recommendations for decorations from the field. After evaluating these recommendations, the Knight Board was to make its recommendations to the Department of the Navy. Secretary Daniels reviewed the board's recommendations and modified them as he saw fit, to include adding the names of individuals who had not been previously submitted to the Knight Board. In a letter to the Senate Committee on Naval Affairs dated December 19, 1919,

Daniels justified this practice by saying, "...I desire to emphasize the fact that this board of awards was established by my order and its recommendations were only for the information of the Secretary of the Navy. The board, therefore, did not have any statutory authority, its recommendations were not final, and the executive was authorized to act as if no board had been constituted. There is nothing to prevent the Secretary of the Navy from departing from the recommendations of this board when in his opinion this should be done."

One of Secretary Daniels' most controversial moves was to award the Distinguished Service Medal to those officers in command of ships sunk by enemy attack and whose "conduct was meritorious in such cases." Daniels awarded the Distinguished Service Medal to ten commanding officers whose ships were either sunk or seriously damaged by enemy submarines or mines. This group of awards was bitterly criticized by Admiral William S. Sims, who had commanded the U.S. Navy forces in Europe. Sims wrote that he felt "... impelled to invite attention to a special class of awards which are the subject of such severe condemnation and ridicule that the effect upon the present and future morale of the service must necessarily be deplorable to the last degree - namely, the Distinguished Service Medals awarded to many, if not all, of the officers who were defeated in action, or whose ships were sunk or seriously damaged by enemy submarines...." Sims went on to note that "The commanding officer of a vessel that is sunk by a submarine should not receive the same award as the commanding officer of a vessel which sinks a submarine."

Secretary Daniels, also on his own initiative and without any recommendations from their commanding officers, awarded fifteen Distinguished Service Medals to enlisted men whose service he considered to be sufficiently heroic as to justify an award of the Distinguished Service Medal.

After the outbreak of World War II the laws governing the award of naval decorations were changed and the ambiguities in precedence were eliminated. Public Law 702 of August 7, 1942, placed the Navy Cross above the Distinguished Service Medal and restricted it to acts of extraordinary heroism. The Distinguished Service Medal was designated as an award solely for outstanding performance of duty in a position of high responsibility. The Navy Distinguished Service Medal is currently awarded to any person who, while serving in any capacity with the Navy or Marine Corps, distinguishes himself by exceptionally meritorious service to the United States in a duty of great responsibility. To justify this decoration, an exceptional performance of duty, clearly above that normally expected, which has contributed materially to the success of a major command or project is required. In general, the

Distinguished Service Medal will be awarded only to those officers in principal commands at sea whose service is such as to justify the award. However, Navy regulations provide that this emphasis shall not be interpreted to preclude the award of the Distinguished Service Medal to any individual whose service meets the requirements.

To secure a proper design for the new Distinguished Service Medal, the Navy applied to its Division of Pictorial Publicity. The Division in turn sought the assistance of Paul Manship, a distinguished sculptor. Manship's design was simple, yet striking. It is a gilded bronze medallion; on its obverse, in the center of the medallion, appears an American bald eagle with its wings spread. In its talons the eagle holds an olive branch and arrows, alluding to distinguished service in both peace and war. The eagle is surrounded by a blue enameled annulet which contains the words, *UNITED STATES OF AMERICA NAVY*, with the *NAVY* centered at

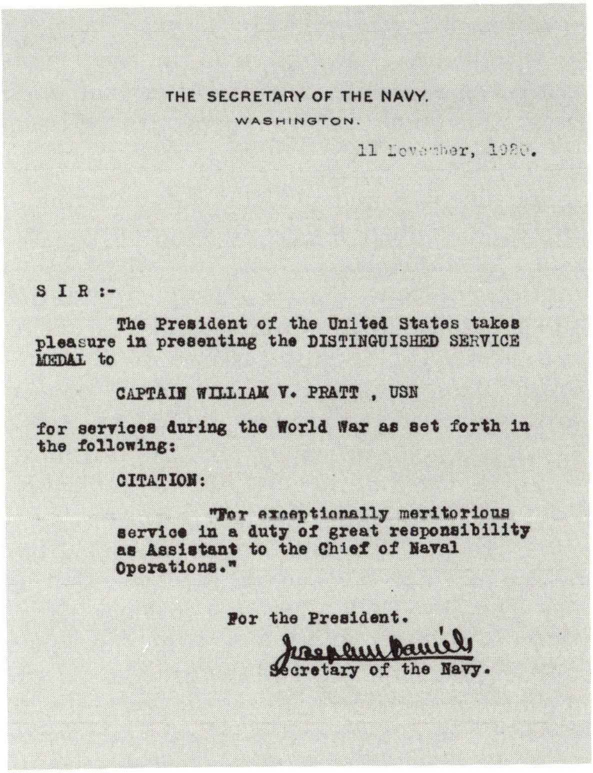

THE SECRETARY OF THE NAVY.
WASHINGTON.

11 November, 1920.

S I R :-

The President of the United States takes pleasure in presenting the DISTINGUISHED SERVICE MEDAL to

CAPTAIN WILLIAM V. PRATT , USN

for services during the World War as set forth in the following:

CITATION:

"For exceptionally meritorious service in a duty of great responsibility as Assistant to the Chief of Naval Operations."

For the President.

Josephus Daniels
Secretary of the Navy.

Letter of transmittal from Secretary of the Navy Josephus Daniels awarding the Navy Distinguished Service Medal to Captain William V. Pratt, USN. (US Navy photo) the bottom of the annulet. On the outside of the annulet is a gold border with a design of scroll waves. In his original design, Manship had the medal suspended from a bar (in the shape of a warship in profile) and suspender (two stylized dolphins). This unique bar was dropped in favor of a white enameled five-pointed star having an anchor in the center. The star is tipped on each point with a gold ball and has gold rays emitting from its re-entrant angles. The obverse design of the Navy Distinguished Service Medal is conceptually similar to that of the Army Distinguished Service Medal (the central theme in both is an eagle surrounded by a blue enameled annulet). In spite of these similarities, the Navy Distinguished Service Medal is distinctive in its own right.

The reverse of the Distinguished Service Medal shows a trident in the center, surmounted by a wreath of laurel. The wreath is in turn surrounded by a blue enameled annulet which contains the inscription *FOR DISTINGUISHED SERVICE.* The trident is the symbol of the authority of Poseidon, the Greek god of the sea who had the power to cause earthquakes (in Roman mythology, Poseidon is known as Neptune). The ribbon to the Navy Distinguished Service Medal is navy blue with a one quarter inch wide stripe of gold in the center (this combination represents the Navy's official colors).

The Manship design was accepted by the Commission on Fine Arts; however, the acceptance was subsequently withdrawn in favor of a design by James E. Fraser, submitted by the firm of Whitehead and Hoag of Newark, New Jersey. Interestingly, at the time Fraser was a member of the Commission on Fine Arts (which had the responsibility for deciding which design would be accepted). The Fraser design is a bronze medallion. In its center is an anchor with a line secured at its top, fouled on its shank, and terminating in the anchor's left fluke. Behind the right fluke is a spray of laurel, and in the distance behind the anchor is a horizon of sea with a setting sun in the upper left quarter of the medal. Forming an arc above the anchor is the inscription, *FOR DISTINGUISHED SERVICE.* The medal is suspended by an eagle whose wings are spread so they extend to the edges of the ribbon. In the eagle's talons is a scroll which bears the inscription, "1917-1918." Although the Fraser design was approved and one hundred and seven of the medals were actually manufactured by Whitehead and Hoag, the medals were found to be unsatisfactory by the Navy and approval for the design was withdrawn. The Manship design was re-accepted and remains the design for the Navy Distinguished Service Medal.

As is the case with the distinguished service medals of the other services, the Distinguished Service Medal is the highest award the Navy can confer upon its personnel for outstanding performance in a duty of great responsibility. For this reason it is sparingly given and almost always goes to flag-rank officers of either the Navy or Marine Corps. Prior to the establishment of the Defense Distinguished Service Medal, the Navy Distinguished Service Medal was occasionally awarded to high ranking Army or Air Force officers who held unified commands which included subordinate Navy elements.

The first Navy Distinguished Service Medal was awarded posthumously to Brigadier General Charles M. Doyen, USMC.

obverse

First Navy Distinguished Service Medal. Although it was never officially approved, examples of this version occasionally seen. (Photo by R.E. Fischer)

reverse

THE DISTINGUISHED SERVICE MEDAL

(U.S. Air Force)

The Air Force Distinguished Service Medal is a "descendant" of the Army Distinguished Service Medal. When the Air Force became a separate branch of the armed forces in 1947, it continued to award Army decorations. Since the Air Force had formerly been a part of the Army, it retained the right to award decorations which had been authorized for the Army, but awarded them under Air Force authority. In time the Air Force was granted authority to award its own design of these decorations and accordingly established its own versions. Thus, the authority which created the Air Force Distinguished Service Medal was the Act of Congress of July 9, 1918 (which created the original Distinguished Service Medal); however, the legislation authorizing an Air Force version was Public Law 86-593 of July 6, 1960. The effective date of the Air Force Distinguished Service Medal was November 1, 1965. A member of the Air Force who was awarded a Distinguished Service Medal before that date received the Army version,

Like the Distinguished Service Medals of the other service branches, the Air Force Distinguished Service Medal is awarded for exceptionally meritorious service to the United States in a duty of great responsibility. A first award of an Air Force Distinguished Service Medal may be made on the basis of a completed period of outstanding service in a position of great responsibility; however, subsequent awards (excluding an award at the time of retirement) are restricted to extraordinary, specific achievements during one or more periods of service. In wartime, a duty of great responsibility is defined as one that involves the exercise of authority or judgment in matters that decide the successful operation of a major command, activity, installation, or program.

Because of the nature of the requirements for an Air Force Distinguished Service Medal, it is seldom awarded to anyone below the rank of brigadier general. In those rare instances when it is awarded to an officer of lesser rank, it is usually a retirement award to a colonel who held a position of unusually great responsibility.

The Air Force Distinguished Service Medal was designed by Frank Alston of the Army's Institute of Heraldry, and represents a radical departure in basic design from the other Distinguished Service Medals. The obverse is a sunburst of thirteen gold rays separated by thirteen white enameled stars. The medal itself is two and a quarter inches in diameter. In the center of the sunburst is a blue stone. The reverse of the medal is blank. The ring of thirteen

obverse

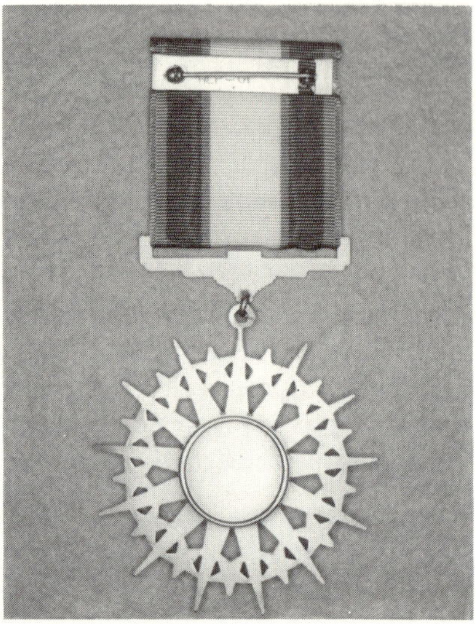

reverse

USAF Distinguished Service Medal

rays and stars symbolize both the thirteen original colonies as well as man's endless chain of achievement. The sunburst itself represents the burst of glory that goes with high achievement, while the sun rays allude to man's constant quest for knowledge. The stars also symbolize the high ideals of achievement and the lofty purpose of the medal itself. The blue stone in the center represents the vault of the heavens and alludes to the operational environment of the Air Force. The medal is suspended from its ribbon by a bar which consists of a set of stylized wings which are symbolic of the Air Force. The ribbon has a stripe of white in the center bordered on both sides by a stripe of Old Gold; a stripe of ultramarine, and a wide stripe of Old Gold.

Interestingly enough, the present design of the Air Force Distinguished Service Medal was not the original approved design for this decoration. The original design, like the other service Distinguished Service Medals, was round and had an eagle in the center. This original design was modified slightly and accepted as the final design of the Airman's Medal.

obverse

reverse

USCG Distinguished Service Medal

THE DISTINGUISHED SERVICE MEDAL

(U.S. Coast Guard)

The United States Coast Guard had virtually no decorations of its own from its inception through World War II. Even the Gold and Silver Lifesaving Medals, which are administered by the Coast Guard, are not themselves Coast Guard decorations. During time of war or when the Coast Guard serves under Navy auspices, its members receive Navy decorations. Although this arrangement was satisfactory through World War II, Coast Guard officials felt that distinctive decorations were appropriate and initiated efforts to secure permission to obtain them.

In 1949 this effort bore fruit when the Coast Guard sought and received the authority to award its own Distinguished Service Medal, thus giving it the means for providing a suitable reward for outstanding service to the United States in a purely Coast Guard capacity. The Coast Guard Distinguished Service Medal was officially established by Act of Congress on August 4, 1949 (Title 14, U.S. Code, section 492).

The Coast Guard Distinguished Service Medal is awarded to any person who, while serving in any capacity with the Coast Guard, distinguishes himself or herself by exceptionally meritorious service to the United States in a duty of great responsibility. To justify an award of the Distinguished Service Medal, an exceptional performance of duty, clearly above that normally expected, which has contributed materially to the success of a major command or project, is required. In general, the Coast Guard Distinguished Service Medal is normally awarded only to those officers in principal commands whose service is such as to justify the award. However, Coast Guard regulations clearly provide that "this is not necessarily interpreted to preclude award of the Coast Guard Distinguished Service Medal to any individual whose service meets the requirements." If there is any doubt as to the degree of service involved, the Legion of Merit is considered the more appropriate decoration. The Secretary of Transportation has retained the authority to approve, in the name of the President, all awards of the Coast Guard Distinguished Service Medal.

The Coast Guard Distinguished Service Medal was designed and sculpted by Thomas Hudson Jones of the Army's Institute of Heraldry. It is a gold disc and on its obverse shows a representation of the U.S. Revenue Cutter *Massachusetts* under full sail on a moderate sea. In a circle surrounding the ship are the words, *U.S. COAST GUARD* in the upper portion, and *DISTINGUISHED SERVICE* in the lower. On the reverse is the Coast

Guard Seal above a blank streamer (used for engraving the recipient's name) which follows the contour of the lower half of the medal. The ribbon consists of a central stripe of light blue, bordered on each side by a pinstripe of white. The ribbon is edged in purple.

In terms of its symbolism, the U.S. Revenue Cutter *Massachusetts* was built in 1791 and was the first Revenue Cutter. As the forerunner of a long line of similar vessels which rendered distinguished service to U.S. Maritime history, it was considered to be a fitting symbol to use on the Coast Guard Distinguished Service Medal. The Coast Guard Seal on the reverse alludes to the service branch which awards the medal.

Although the Coast Guard Distinguished Service Medal was authorized in 1949, its design was not approved until February 1, 1961. The first recipient was Admiral Alfred C. Richmond, Commandant of the Coast Guard, who received the medal on October 3, 1961.

First Coast Guard Distinguished Service Medal awarded. Admiral Alfred C. Richmond receives the first Coast Guard Distinguished Service Medal from Secretary of the Treasury Douglas C. Dillon on September 29, 1961. (US Coast Guard photo)

THE SILVER STAR

The Silver Star has evolved over the years from a simple citation for gallantry in action to a major military decoration. It grew out of the practice of citing a soldier in the despatches of the day, a procedure by which a soldier was publicly recognized for some noteworthy action performed during the course of a battle.

The formal practice of using the daily despatches to cite soldiers of all ranks for gallantry in action was probably started by the British in 1843 during the Scinde Campaign against Afghan rebels. During the First World War, the French established the Croix de Guerre on April 8, 1915, to commemorate individuals whose feats of arms were mentioned in the despatches from the commander of an army, corps, division, brigade or regiment. The person cited in the despatches was authorized to wear the Croix de Guerre, and the level of the despatch was indicated by a device (a palm or a star) attached to the ribbon of the medal. Belgium followed suit on October 25, 1915, by instituting its own Croix de Guerre which was also used to recognize a mention in the despatches. Although the British used the "mention in the despatches" as a means for recognizing gallantry, they did not issue a medal to the recipient of the "MID." However, in 1920 they did authorize a multi-leaved bronze oak leaf to be worn on the ribbon of the Victory Medal by those who had received a MID during the First World War.

The practice of using a mention in the despatches to cite gallantry in action was likewise adopted by the United States Army during the First World War. On July 9, 1918, Congress passed a law which provided for a small silver star (three sixteenths of an inch in circumscribing diameter) to be worn on the ribbon of the appropriate campaign medal by any officer or enlisted man who had been cited in orders for gallantry in action under conditions not warranting the award of a Medal of Honor or Distinguished Service Cross. This "Citation Star" was not limited to the First World War, but could be granted for citations made during earlier wars as well. In the case of the First World War, the Citation Star was to be worn on the ribbon of the Victory Medal. The citation itself had to be in orders issued from the headquarters of a force commanded by a general officer and had to be for gallantry in action. The Citation Star was not accompanied by any other award; indeed, the star itself was not even presented to the soldier who won it. The mention in the orders was both the justification and authorization for the soldier to procure his own Citation Star.

A similar device was authorized for Navy and Marine Corps personnel. Recognizing that members of the naval service performed numerous acts of gallantry that fell short of the requirements for either a Medal of Honor or a Navy Cross, the Navy issued

obverse

reverse

Silver Star

General Order Number 482 of 1920, paragraph 3 of which authorized a "special letter of commendation" to be awarded upon the recommendation of the Board of Awards. The special letter of commendation was deemed to take place "in the class with, though below, the medals provided by Congress." Receipt of a special letter of commendation authorized its recipient to wear a small silver star on the ribbon of the Victory Medal.

Distinguished Service Cross group to Lt Edgar A. Jennings, who won both the DSC and the Silver Star in World War I. The Silver Star is indicated by the small "Citation Star" above the bars on his Victory Medal (center). The third medal is the French Croix de Guerre.

In 1932 the Silver Star was redesigned as a medal. The "Citation Star" was placed in the center of a larger star-shaped pendant and a ribbon was added. Those who had previously earned a Citation Star were then allowed to apply for the Silver Star medal. After the Second World War broke out, the status of the Silver Star was further clarified. On August 7, 1942, Congress authorized the President to present (but not in the name of Congress) a Silver Star to any person who, while serving in any capacity with the Navy since December 6, 1941, distinguished himself by gallantry and intrepidity in action, but not of a nature to justify the award of a Navy Cross. Four months later, on December 15, 1942, the Silver Star was likewise extended to Army personnel for gallantry in action, but not of a degree to justify an award of the Distinguished Service Cross.

The Silver Star Medal is a gilt-toned bronze star, one and one half inches in circumscribing diameter. In the center of the medal there is a small silver star, three-sixteenths of an inch in circumscribing diameter. This smaller star is centered in a laurel wreath, and there are eighteen rays radiating from the silver star. The reverse of the medal is blank except for the raised inscription, *FOR GALLANTRY IN ACTION.* The star is suspended by a rectangular shaped metal loop with rounded corners, and the medal is suspended from a moired silk ribbon. Symbolically, the star stands for the United States, just as each star in the flag stands for one of the individual states in the Union. The small silver star in the center of the medal represents the original Citation Star, and the wreath which surrounds it represents achievement. The colors of the ribbon are likewise taken from the flag and represent the national colors.

The Silver Star is currently awarded by all branches of the armed forces to any person who, while serving in any capacity, is cited for gallantry in action against an enemy of the United States while engaged in military operations involving conflict with an opposing foreign force, or while serving with friendly forces engaged in armed conflict against an opposing armed force in which the United States is not a belligerent party. The required gallantry, while of a lesser degree than that required for a Medal of Honor, Distinguished Service Cross, Navy Cross, or Air Force Cross, must still have been performed with "marked distinction."

Color Plates

Navy Medal of Honor
(1862 - 1913)

Navy Medal of Honor
(1913 - 1917)

Navy Medal of Honor
(1917 - 1942)

Navy Medal of Honor
(1942 - present)

Army Medal of Honor
(1862 - 1896)

Army Medal of Honor
(1896 - 1904)

Army Medal of Honor
(1904 - 1944)

Army Medal of Honor
(1944 - present)

Air Force Medal of Honor

Brevet Medal

Certificate of Merit Medal

Distinguished Service Cross
(First Style)

Distinguished Service Cross
(Current style)

Navy Cross

Air Force Cross

Defense Distinguished Service Medal

Army Distinguished Service Medal

Navy Distinguished Service Medal
(First - unapproved - version)

Navy Distinguished Service Medal
(Approved version)

USAF Distinguished Service Medal

USCG Distinguished Service Medal

Silver Star

Defense Superior Service Medal

Legion of Merit
(Chief commander)

Legion of Merit
(Commander)

Legion of Merit
(Officer)

Legion of Merit
(Legionnaire)

Specially Meritorious Service Medal, 1898

Gold Lifesaving Medal
(1882 - 1949)

Gold Lifesaving Medal
(1949 - present)

Silver Lifesaving Medal
(1882 - 1949)

Silver Lifesaving Medal
(1949 - present)

Soldier's Medal

Navy & Marine Corps Medal

Airman's Medal

Coast Guard Medal

Distinguished Flying Cross

Bronze Star Medal

Defense Meritorious Service Medal

Meritorious Service Medal

Air Medal

Joint Service Commendation Medal

Army Commendation Medal

Navy Commendation Medal

USAF Commendation Medal

USCG Commendation Medal
(1947 - 1968)

USCG Commendation Medal
(1968 - present)

Navy Achievement Medal

USAF Achievement Medal

Army Achievement Medal

USCG Achievement Medal

Purple Heart Medal

THE DEFENSE SUPERIOR SERVICE MEDAL

In the summer of 1975, William Clements (who was at that time Deputy Secretary of Defense), recommended that a certain Army general then assigned to the Office of the Secretary of Defense be awarded the Legion of Merit upon completion of his tour of duty. The recommendation was forwarded through the appropriate Army channels without any problems, but when it reached the Secretary of the Army, it was turned down.

As a direct result, on September 23, 1975, Clements wrote to William K. Brehm, Assistant Secretary of Defense for Manpower and Reserve Affairs, and told him that there was "a definite requirement" for a new decoration at the Department of Defense level to recognize exceptional performance of duty by members of the Armed Forces who were assigned to the Office of the Secretary of Defense or to other joint activities within the Department of Defense. Clements specifically wanted a medal which "...would recognize duty performed with a distinction and significance that would justify an award comparable to the Legion of Merit...." Mr. Clements' military assistant (a Navy admiral) subsequently provided specific guidance on what was wanted: the new medal was to be called the "Defense Superior Service Medal" and was to be issued under the authority of an Executive Order by the President. The medal was to be obtained at the lowest possible cost and "with as little involvement as possible." For these reasons it was directed that the medal use the same design as that of the Defense Distinguished Service Medal except that it be finished in silver rather than gold and the inscription on the reverse properly modified.

On November 13, 1975, Mr. Clements forwarded a proposed Executive Order for the establishment of the Defense Superior Service Medal for submission to the President for his approval and signature. In this letter, Mr. Clements pointed out that although the Secretaries of the Military Departments had a full range of decorations with which to reward deserving individuals, the Secretary of Defense had only the Defense Distinguished Service Medal and the Joint Service Commendation Medal at his disposal. He pointed out that there was no medal comparable to the Legion of Merit and that such a medal was needed.

Clements formally approved the design of the proposed Defense Superior Service Medal and its ribbon on November 18, 1975, and on February 6, 1976, President Gerald R. Ford signed the proposed Executive Order (EO 11904), formally establishing the Defense Superior Service Medal.

obverse

reverse

Defense Superior Service Medal

The Defense Superior Service Medal is awarded by the Secretary of Defense for exceptionally meritorious service to any military member who is assigned to a joint staff or other joint activity of the Department of Defense. Authority to award the Defense Superior Service Medal cannot be delegated; however, recommendations for its award can be made by appropriate authorities within the service branches. The Defense Superior Service Medal cannot be awarded to any individual for a period of service for which a Legion of Merit or similar decoration is awarded.

The Defense Superior Service Medal is almost identical in design to the Defense Distinguished Service Medal, except that it is silver in color. The medal was designed by Mildred Orloff and sculpted by Lewis J. King, Jr., both of the Army's Institute of Heraldry. It is one and seven-eighths inches in overall height and features a medium-blue enameled pentagon (point up) superimposed by a silver eagle with outspread wings. The eagle's breast is charged with the shield of the United States, and the eagle holds three crossed arrows in its talons. The pentagon and eagle are enclosed within a silver, pierced circle consisting in the upper half of thirteen stars and in the lower half of a wreath of laurel on the left and olive on the right. At the top of the medal is a suspender composed of five graduated silver rays which extend above the stars. On the reverse of the medal, in relief, are the words, *FROM THE SECRETARY OF DEFENSE TO* and *FOR SUPERIOR SERVICE.* The ribbon is composed of a central stripe of red, flanked on either side by stripes of white, blue and gold.

The eagle is taken from the seal of the Secretary of Defense and is the American bald eagle. The pentagon in the background alludes to the Pentagon Building in Washington, D.C., which in turn represents the military services as well as to the office of the Secretary of Defense (all of which are headquartered in the Pentagon). The thirteen stars represent the thirteen colonies, and through them, all of the states. The olive branch represents the goal of defense - peace - while the laurel branch represents achievement.

obverse

reverse

Legion of Merit
(Legionnaire)

THE LEGION OF MERIT

The Legion of Merit is actually a derivative of the original Purple Heart. When George Washington established the Purple Heart on August 7, 1782, it was known as the Badge of Military Merit and was to be awarded for "singularly meritorious action." The Badge of Military Merit was in the shape of a Purple Heart and was only known to have been awarded three times. After the Revolution it fell into disuse for over one hundred and fifty years. On February 22, 1932, it was reinstituted as the Purple Heart medal. The new Purple Heart was to be awarded for wounds received in action but not awarded for any other kind of meritorious performance of duty.

When the United States entered World War II, it was again faced with the problem of not having an adequate range of decorations with which to reward the various kinds and degrees of achievement, nor did it have a multi-level decoration for noncombat achievement comparable to many of the decorations awarded by the European allies. Many of the allies awarded their decorations in "degrees" (e.g., knight, officer, commander, etc). The Legion of Merit was created to fill this gap. On July 20, 1942, Congress authorized the Legion of Merit, to be awarded in four classes, with George Washington's Badge of Military Merit being designated as its legal precursor. In its reconstituted form the Legion of Merit was originally conceived as a decoration comparable to the French Legion of Honor (hence its similarity in both name and appearance). It was intended to be awarded to a wide variety of recipients, including military and civil service personnel, civilians, and foreigners and was to reward outstanding service rendered over a fairly long period of time. It was also intended to be a decoration which could be awarded in different degrees based on the individual's rank and position (if a foreigner) and the magnitude of his contribution, if an American.

At first award of the Legion of Merit was very rigorously controlled: on September 15, 1942, President Roosevelt notified the Secretary of the Navy that all awards of the Legion of Merit were to be submitted to the President for his personal approval. Roosevelt noted that "...during the early awards and until we get the thing running smoothly, I want to keep a personal eye on just what is being done." This procedure was carefully followed; however, it soon became apparent that these procedures were too cumbersome and made the Legion of Merit too restrictive. On January 31, 1943, General George C. Marshall wrote the President and told him that "While I was in Africa General Eisenhower and General Patton both urged on me the importance of permitting the prompt award to U.S. military personnel of the Legion of Merit." General Marshall pointed out that there were many instances of outstanding performance of duty which did not come up to the standards set for the Distinguished Service Medal but which still deserved a prompt award and that the Legion of Merit was appropriate in such cases.

On February 15, 1943, President Roosevelt replied to General Marshall, stating "I entirely approve the award of the Legion of Merit to U.S. military personnel in the field without further reference to me." The President was emphatic, however, that "The Legion of Merit grades are not to be awarded on the basis of rank but must be awarded as a result of an evaluation of the degree of performance." The problem of awarding the Legion of Merit in various grades to U.S. military personnel continued to create confusion, and on May 26, 1943, the Secretaries of War and Navy sent a joint letter to President Roosevelt recommending that the Legion of Merit be awarded to U.S. military personnel without reference to degree but that it continue to be awarded to foreign recipients according to degree. The President concurred, establishing a policy which remains in effect to this day.

In spite of the intentions of those who created the Legion of Merit, it has ultimately became a military decoration. With respect to military recipients, it was originally intended that it be awarded regardless of rank, so long as the recipient performed exceptionally meritorious service. In fact, the War Department stated that it particularly wanted the Legion of Merit to be awarded to personnel in the enlisted and lower commissioned grades. However, as of June 30, 1947, only 26.14 percent of the Army's 20,273 recipients of the Legion of Merit were either enlisted or in the lower commissioned grades. Only 10.5 percent of the Navy's 4,066 awards of the Legion of Merit went to either enlisted personnel or junior officers.

Since World War II the Legion of Merit has been continuously upgraded. This has resulted at least in part because of the establishment of the various commendation medals and the Meritorious Service Medal. In addition, it has come to be believed that in order to render "exceptionally meritorious conduct in the performance of outstanding service to the United States," the recipient must occupy a position of great responsibility. This means - in actual practice - that a recipient would normally be a fairly high ranking officer. Today, the Legion of Merit is typically awarded to full colonels (and Navy captains) but more often, to generals and admirals.

The Legion of Merit is awarded in four degrees. Only the lowest degree (Legionnaire) can be awarded to a member of the United States armed forces; the higher degrees are reserved for award to foreign recipients. The highest degree is that of Chief Commander, which is awarded to chiefs of state or heads of government. The medal for the degree of Chief Commander is a plaque which is worn on the left breast. The second highest degree is that of Commander and is awarded to foreign recipients who are the equivalent of a U.S. chief of staff or higher, but who are not a head of state. The medal in this degree is worn around the neck. The degree of Officer is awarded to (1) generals or admirals below the equivalent of a U.S. chief of staff, (2) to ranks parallel to colonel for service in assignments equivalent to those usually held by generals in the U.S. military service, and (3) to foreign attaches. The degree of Officer is worn as a breast decoration and is denoted by a miniature of the medal on the suspension ribbon. The degree of Legionnaire is awarded to all other eligible personnel.

Legion of Merit
(Chief commander)

Legion of Merit
(Commander)

When awarded to United States personnel, it must be based on exceptional conduct in the performance of meritorious service to the United States. During peacetime, awards to United States military personnel are generally limited to (1) recognizing service in an extremely difficult duty of national or international significance that is performed in a clearly exceptional manner, (2) service that has aided the United States in furthering its national policies, or (3) service that has furthered the interests or security of the United States or any of its allies during a period of national emergency declared by either the President or the Congress.

Legion of Merit
(Officer)

The Legion of Merit was designed by Colonel Townsend Heard of the U.S. Army and was sculpted by Katherine W. Lane. The medal is a five-pointed American white star of heraldic form and is bordered in purple-red enamel. In the center of the star is a circle of clouds surrounding a field of blue charged with thirteen white stars. Backing the star in its re-entrant angles is a laurel wreath and in each re-entrant angle there are two crossed arrows pointing outward. The reverse of the medal bears the inscription, *UNITED STATES OF AMERICA*, and within a central disc, *ANNUIT COEPTIS* MDCCLXXXII. The ribbon is essentially the same as that of the Purple Heart, with the exception that it is less purple and more red.

In terms of its symbolism, the five arms represent the five-pointed American star. The thirteen white stars on the field of blue are taken from the coat of arms of the United States and represent the thirteen original colonies (and through them, all of the states in the Union). The crossed arrows represent the use of armed force for the protection of the Nation. The color of the ribbon derives from the original Badge of Miliary Merit but is shaded to distinguish it from the ribbon of the Purple Heart.

The first Legion of Merit in the degree of Legionnaire was awarded to a Navy nurse, Lieutenant (junior grade) Ann Agnes Bernatitus, the only member of the Navy medical staff to escape under fire from Bataan and Corregidor. The first recipients of the Legion of Merit in the degree of Officer were Colonel Johanes K. Meijer of the Royal Netherlands Army; Major Herbert J. Thompson of the British Army; and Major Stephan M. Dombrowalski of the Polish Army. The first recipient fo the Legion of Merit in the grade of Commander was Brigadier General Amaro Soares Bittencourt of Brazil, who received the medal on November 8, 1942, from its designer, Col. Heard. The first recipient of the Legion of Merit in the degree of Chief Commander was Generalissimo Chiang Kai-Shek.

When the Legion of Merit was first manufactured in the early 1940's it was numbered so a record could be kept indicating which medal went to which recipient. The practice was soon discontinued and has not been revived. In addition, very early examples of the Legion of Merit indicate that the space between the arrows in the re-entrant angles of the cross were pierced. This practice was also discontinued as it slowed the production of the medals and added to their cost.

THE DISTINGUISHED FLYING CROSS

Most military decorations are designed to reward a specific degree of heroism or achievement. Although the same is true of the Distinguished Flying Cross, it is also unique in that it rewards heroism or achievement within a specific physical environment -- the air. It is specifically and unmistakably an aviation award.

The Distinguished Flying Cross may be thought of as a product of the First World War. That conflict saw the employment of many new techniques of war, including such devices as poison gas, the flame thrower, tanks and military aircraft. Military aviation not only came into its own during the First World War, it also provided a new arena for feats of valor. The flyers who operated the early military aircraft not only had to be skilled pilots, they also had to have considerable courage and endurance. It is not surprising that new decorations should have emerged which rewarded the achievements of aviators.

The first of these new aviation decorations did not originate in the United States, however. By Royal Warrant dated June 3, 1918, the British Crown created a set of decorations which rewarded aviators for both combat and noncombat heroism (in keeping with British custom, different decorations were created for officers and enlisted personnel). One of these decorations was the Distinguished Flying Cross, awarded to officers who performed noteworthy acts of heroism while engaged against an enemy. The counterpart for enlisted aviators was the Distinguished Flying Medal. For noncombat heroism, officers were awarded the Air Force Cross while enlisted members received the Air Force Medal.

The United States did not create any comparable decorations during the First World War, but rather rewarded aviation heroism and achievement with existing decorations: the Medal of Honor, Distinguished Service Cross, Navy Cross, and in the case of the Navy, occasionally with a Navy Distinguished Service Medal. However, the rapid growth of both civil and military aviation in the immediate postwar years indicated the need for some kind of specific aviation decoration. This need was met on July 2, 1926, when Congress authorized the Distinguished Flying Cross for award to "...any person, who, while serving in any capacity with the Air Corps of the Army, Navy and Marine Corps of the United States, including the National Guard and Organized Reserves, subsequent to 6 April 1917, has distinguished himself by heroism or extraordinary achievement while participating in aerial flight." The Distinguished Flying Cross was thus made retroactive to cover acts performed during the First World War. It was also the first decoration authorized in identical design and ribbon for issue by all

obverse

reverse

Distinguished Flying Cross

branches of the armed forces. The question of whether or not the Distinguished Flying Cross could be awarded to civilians (as it had been to aviation pioneer Amelia Earhart, among others) was resolved on March 1, 1927, when Executive Order 4601 prohibited such awards.

The Distinguished Flying Cross is still awarded by all branches of the armed forces for either heroism or outstanding achievement while participating in aerial flight. The performance of heroism must be evidenced by voluntary action above and beyond the call of duty. If the award is based on outstanding achievement, it must have resulted in an accomplishment so exceptional and outstanding as to clearly set the individual apart from his comrades or from other individuals in similar circumstances.

The Distinguished Flying Cross was designed by Elizabeth Will and Arthur E. DuBois, both of whom were employees of the Army's Institute of Heraldry, and is based on the design of the British Distinguished Flying Cross. The obverse is a bronze cross pattee with a four-bladed propeller superimposed over the cross. In the reentrant angles of the cross are a series of rays which form a one inch square background. The reverse of the medal is plain. The medal is suspended from a plain bar. The ribbon consists of a red stripe in the center, flanked on both sides by white pinstripes which are in turn bordered by a broad stripe of blue. Just inside the outer edges of the ribbon are stripes of white, equal in size to the red stripe in the center.

The cross, which is the ancient symbol for sacrifice, was blended with a very modern symbol - the propeller - to signify that the Distinguished Flying Cross is an award for services rendered while engaged in aerial flight. The ribbon represents the national colors, which are arranged in a combination which distinguishes the ribbon of the Distinguished Flying Cross from all other ribbons using the same colors. Early issues of the Distinguished Flying Cross were serially numbered on the reverse of the lower arm; later issues were serially numbered on the lower edge of the medal. The practice of numbering Distinguished Flying Crosses was discontinued during World War II.

The first award of the Distinguished Flying Cross went to Charles A. Lindbergh (who was a captain in the Army Reserve) for his epic transatlantic flight in 1927; however, the earliest act for which a Distinguished Flying Cross was awarded took place on December 17, 1903, at Kitty Hawk, North Carolina. By Act of Congress on December 18, 1928, Orville and Wilbur Wright were both awarded the Distinguished Flying Cross for that first powered flight. The first Navy recipient of the Distinguished Flying Cross was Commander Richard E. Byrd, who received the Distinguished Flying Cross on May 9, 1926, for his flight to and from the North Pole.

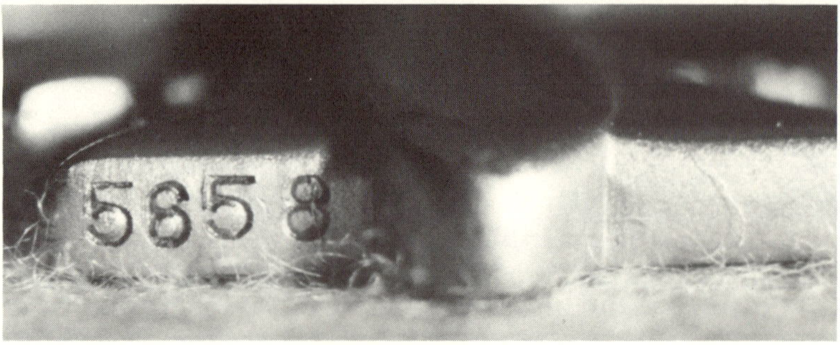

Close-up view of the numbering on the bottom edge of Distinguished Flying Cross 5658.

An early award of the Distinguished Flying Cross. By Act of Congress on May 2, 1928, the DFC was awarded to (from left to right) Baron Gunther von Huenefeld of Germany; Major James Fitzmaurice, Chief of the Irish Free State Air Force; and to Captain Hermann Koehl, German Army (retired). The three won the DFC for making the first westward nonstop transatlantic flight from Europe to North America (April 12-13, 1928). Notice that Major Fitzmaurice has no arms.

First winners of the Distinguished Flying Cross. LCDR Richard E. Byrd (center, in uniform) and Captain Charles A. Lindberg (center, to the right of Byrd). The others in the picture are, from left to right, Edward P. Warner (Assistant Secretary of the Navy for Aviation); W.T. McCracken (Assistant Secretary of War for Aviation); Byrd and Lindberg; Army Air Secretary Davidson, and Third Assistant Postmaster Glover. The photo was taken at the Mayflower Hotel in Washington, D.C. in 1927.

Gold Lifesaving Medal
(1949 - present)

Silver Lifesaving Medal
(1949 - present)

THE GOLD AND SILVER LIFESAVING MEDALS

(United States Coast Guard)

The perils of the sea have been known and feared throughout man's recorded history; however, drowning, shipwreck, and other water related dangers have also been the occasion for notable acts of heroism. Many men and women have sought to save their fellow man from these disasters and many have lost their own lives in the process. Such disasters have not been uncommon in the United States, given the fact that this nation has an extensive coastline and U.S. waters are (and have been) used extensively for both commerce and pleasure.

In 1844 Congress appropriated $5000 to be used by the Department of the Treasury to establish lifesaving stations along the coasts. These stations were manned by volunteers until 1871, when full-time crews were hired. In 1878 Congress created the U.S. Lifesaving Service and placed it under the Treasury Department. The Lifesaving Service worked closely with the Revenue Cutter Service until January 28, 1915, when the two organizations were merged to form the United States Coast Guard.

The U.S. Lifesaving Service had a distinguished history during the 43 years of its existence. It gave aid to 28,121 ships in distress and to 178,741 persons whose lives were in peril. Their rescues often called for taking to rough seas in small boats to attempt rescues under the most difficult of circumstances. It is not surprising, therefore, that in order to recognize such heroism Congress created a set of lifesaving medals on June 20, 1874.

These medals were originally known as the *Lifesaving Medal First Class (Gold)* and the *Lifesaving Medal Second Class (Silver).* They were authorized for presentation to those who rescued or attempted to rescue individuals who were in danger of drowning in waters within the United States or under its jurisdiction (if the act took place outside of such waters, at least one of the parties involved had to have been a United States citizen).

Since the merger of the Revenue Cutter Service and the United States Lifesaving Service in 1915, the United States Coast Guard has continued to perform a search and rescue role; therefore it is logical and proper that the administration of the Lifesaving Medals remains under the authority of the Commandant of the U.S. Coast Guard. Over the years, the sea rescue function has become increasingly sophisticated and all of the military services (including the Coast Guard) now have their own decorations for non-combat heroism, making the Gold and Silver Lifesaving Medals essentially civilian decorations.

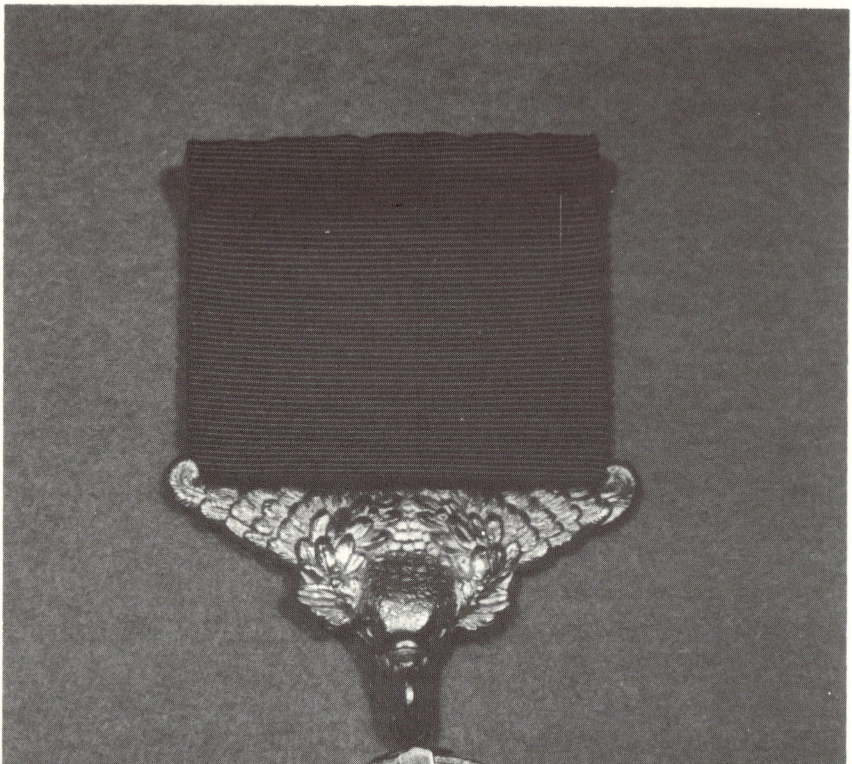

Gold Lifesaving Medal
(1882 - 1949)

THE GOLD LIFESAVING MEDAL

The Gold Lifesaving Medal was designed by Anthony C. Paquet, who at the time was the Chief Engraver at the Philadelphia Mint. The original Gold Lifesaving Medal was not intended to be worn; it was a so-called "table medal." It was one and three-fourths inches in circumference and was struck in 99.9% pure gold. The obverse of the medal shows three men in a boat in a heavy sea. One of the men is rowing the boat while another is standing, preparing to throw a line. The third figure is reaching out to help a fourth figure, a mariner in distress who is clinging to a spar. In the distance (to the left) is the wreck of a ship. The whole is surrounded by the words, *LIFESAVING MEDAL OF THE FIRST CLASS* in the upper half and, *UNITED STATES OF AMERICA* in the lower half. The two inscriptions are separated by small five-pointed stars.

The reverse contains an ornate monument. An American eagle with displayed wings is perched atop the monument, and to its left is the figure of a woman holding an oak wreath in her left hand, and with her right hand she is preparing to inscribe the name of the recipient on the monument. To the right of the monument are grouped a mast, a yard with a sail, an anchor, a sextant, and a spray of laurel. Under the monument, in two lines, are the words, *ACT OF CONGRESS JUNE 20th 1874.* The whole is surrounded by the words, *IN TESTIMONY OF HEROIC DEEDS IN SAVING LIFE FROM THE PERILS OF THE SEA.*

On June 18, 1878, Congress made some minor changes in the design of the medal. The words, *LIFESAVING MEDAL OF THE FIRST CLASS* were removed from the upper half of the obverse and replaced with *UNITED STATES OF AMERICA*, taken from the lower half, which was in turn replaced by *ACT OF CONGRESS JUNE 20, 1874*, which was removed from the reverse of the medal.

The Gold Lifesaving Medal was again modified, this time by Act of Congress of May 4, 1882, when it was fitted with a suspension device and a ribbon. The suspension device is a gold eagle's head (as seen from above) and outstretched wings (which form the suspender through which the ribbon is passed). The ribbon was red and was two inches wide. Outside of these relatively minor alterations, the medal remained essentially unchanged.

reverse

On March 13, 1946, Admiral J.F. Farley, who was then Commandant of the Coast Guard, sent a memorandum to the Secretary of the Treasury in which he proposed several changes to the lifesaving medals. He suggested that their respective ribbons be changed because they were easily confused with the ribbons to other medals. The Gold Lifesaving Medal ribbon was similar to those of the Specially Meritorious Service Medal, 1898, and of the Navy Good Conduct Medal. He also recommended that the size of the medals be reduced to enable them to "...present a more harmonious appearance when they are worn on the uniform with other medals...." The suggestions were approved by the Secretary of the Treasury on April 4, 1949, and made official by Act of Congress on August 4, 1949. The revised Lifesaving Medals were one and seven-sixteenths inches in diameter and the Gold Lifesaving Medal was struck in 99.9% pure gold. The only change to the medal itself (other than to reduce it in size) was that the inscription on the lower obverse was changed to *ACT OF CONGRESS AUGUST 4, 1949.* The ribbon was changed to one and three-eighths inches in width and consists of a a center stripe of gold bordered on either side by a stripe of white and edged with a stripe of red.

The Gold Lifesaving Medal may be awarded to any person who rescues or endeavors to rescue any other person from drowning, shipwreck, or other peril of the water. The rescue or attempted rescue must take place in waters within the United States or subject to the jurisdiction thereof, or if the rescue or attempted rescue takes place outside of such waters, one or the other of the parties must be a citizen of the United States or from a vessel or aircraft owned or operated by citizens of the United States. In order to qualify for the Gold Lifesaving Medal, the rescue or attempted rescue must be made at the risk of one's own life and must evince extreme and heroic daring.

THE SILVER LIFESAVING MEDAL

The Silver Lifesaving Medal was also designed by Anthony C. Paquet, and was likewise originally a table medal. It was one and three-fourths inches in diameter and was struck from 99.9% pure silver. The obverse of the medal shows a man struggling in a heavy sea; hovering above him is the figure of a woman who is offering him one end of a long scarf. The whole is encircled by the words, *LIFESAVING MEDAL OF THE SECOND CLASS* in the upper half, and *UNITED STATES OF AMERICA* in the lower half. The two halves are separated by small five-pointed stars. The reverse contains a large wreath of laurel knotted at the bottom with a

Silver Lifesaving Medal
(1882 - 1949)

reverse

flowing ribbon. Within the wreath at the top are the words, *ACT OF CONGRESS JUNE 20th 1874.* The whole is encircled by the words, *IN TESTIMONY OF HEROIC DEEDS IN SAVING LIFE FROM THE PERILS OF THE SEA.* There is a small decorative scroll at the bottom of the medal.

The Act of Congress on June 18, 1878, which modified the Gold Lifesaving Medal also modified the Silver Lifesaving Medal. The obverse was altered to replace the words, *LIFESAVING MEDAL OF THE SECOND CLASS* with *UNITED STATES OF AMERICA,* taken from the lower half. The latter was replaced with *ACT OF CONGRESS JUNE 20th 1874,* which was removed from the reverse of the medal. The two small five-pointed stars were also removed from the obverse of the medal.

In 1882 the Silver Lifesaving Medal was again modified, this time to add a silver suspension bar (of the same design as that of the Gold Lifesaving Medal) and to add a light blue two-inch wide ribbon. The final modification of the Silver Lifesaving Medal occurred in 1949 at the same time and under the same circumstances the Gold Lifesaving Medal was changed. The current Silver Lifesaving Medal was reduced in size to one and seven-sixteenths of an inch in diameter and is struck from 99% pure silver. The date on the inscription on the obverse was changed to *AUGUST 4, 1949* and the ribbon reduced in width to one and three-eighths inches. The ribbon is composed of a center stripe of silver-gray, bordered by a stripe of white and edged with a stripe of blue.

The Silver Lifesaving Medal is awarded under the same conditions as the Gold Lifesaving Medal, except that the act need not involve the degree of heroism and risk called for in the case of the Gold Lifesaving Medal.

Additional awards of a Gold or Silver Lifesaving Medal are denoted by ornate bars which are inscribed with the recipient's name. The bar is made of the same metal as the medal. The bars are plain and horizontal. The tail of a flowing ribbon is draped over the left end of the bar; the ribbon then passes behind the bar and emerges underneath, flowing upward toward the center of the bar and then downward, ending just below and before the right end of the bar. On the ribbon are the words, *ACT OF CONGRESS AUGUST 4, 1949.* The bar and ribbon are nestled in a spray of laurel which shows above and below the bar.

obverse

reverse

Specially Meritorious Service Medal, 1898

THE SPECIALLY MERITORIOUS SERVICE MEDAL, 1898

(U.S. Navy - Obsolete)

During the Spanish-American War (1898), a number of Navy and Marine Corps personnel performed acts of heroism other than in battle, even though those acts may have taken place in an area in which a battle was raging. These acts were not deemed worthy of a Medal of Honor, which was the only decoration available at the time. However, the Navy did wish to offer some form of recognition for these acts. As a result, on March 3, 1901, Congress passed Public Resolution 17 which provided among other things that a "specially meritorious service medal" was to be given to all officers and men of the Navy and Marine Corps who rendered heroic and conspicuous service, other than in battle, during the Spanish-American War.

This was a unique decoration for two reasons. First, its use was limited to the Spanish-American War. Second, it was not normally given for isolated, individual acts of heroism. It was given to individuals who, as members of a group, performed some note-worthy action. It has generally been accepted that 93 Specially Meritorious Service Medals were awarded to members of the boat crews who saved the lives of Spanish sailors who had jumped from their burning ships - their citations reading, *RESCUING CREWS FROM AND IN CLOSE PROXIMITY TO BURNING SHIPS AFTER THE BATTLE OFF SANTIAGO, CUBA, JULY 3RD, 1898.* The names of 71 of the rescuing crews were listed in a letter of January 30, 1904, ordering their medals to be engraved by the United States Mint. Those recipients included the following:

USS INDIANA

Ensign Percy N. Olmstead

Naval Cadet Frank P. Helm, Jr.

Assistant Surgeon George D. Costigan

Chaplain Percy G. Cassard

Captain Littleton W.T. Waller, USMC

USS IOWA

Ensign Nathan C. Twining

Naval Cadet Arthur J. Hepburn

John Clune, Coxwain

John W.M. Moseley, Coxwain

James Treinor, Coxwain
William Allen, Seaman
Daniel H. Murphy, Seaman
Stephen Nolan, Seaman
Emil Totterman, Seaman
John Casey, Ordinary Seaman
Robert Walsh, Apprentice 1st Class
Carl H. George, Apprentice 2nd Class
Joseph M. Murphy, Apprentice 2nd Class

USS GLOUCESTER

Lieutenant Thomas G Wood
Lieutenant (junior grade) George H. Norman
Ensign John T. Edson
Assistant Engineer Andre M. Procter
William H. Sellers, Chief Yeoman
William G. Bee, Chief Gunner's Mate
John Bond Chief Boatswain's Mate
George Chipman, Electrician 1st Class
George B. Evans, Quartermaster 1st Class
Patrick Kay, Ship's Cook 1st Class
Peter Keller, Boatswain's Mate 1st Class
Hans Dahl, Coxwain
Adam Jaggi, Coxwain
Patrick Lynch, Coxwain
Neil H. Lykke, Seaman Gunner
Otto Brown, Seaman
Carl A. Collin, Seaman
Alvin D. Thompson, Seaman
Martin J. Tierney, Seaman
Frank Wirtane, Seaman
Richard Daly, Ordinary Seaman
Oscar Halvorson, Ordinary Seaman
Samuel Kastell, Ordinary Seaman

William M. Lawrence, Ordinary Seaman
John W. Lewis, Ordinary Seaman
Thomas Macklin, Ordinary Seaman
Griffith Roberts, Ordinary Seaman
Charles Rozzle, Ordinary Seaman
Michael Magee, Painter
John Cooksey, Landsman
Milo K. Davis, Landsman
Bernard Loehrs, Landsman
Louis Quentin, Landsman

USS HARVARD

Lieutenant Joseph Beale
Lieutenant (junior grade) Archibald H. Davis
Naval Cadet John Halligan, Jr.
Paul D. Mills, Gunner's Mate 2nd Class
Max L. Scull, Gunner's Mate 3rd Class
James A. McGreger, Seaman
Arthur J. Amundsen, Ordinary Seaman
Arling R. Hansen, Ordinary Seaman
C. Earle Skeen, Ordinary Seaman

USS HIST

Lieutenant (junior grade) Felix H. Hunicke
Assistant Engineer Edward S. Kellogg
August H. Brown, Chief Yeoman
Edward J. Bourke, Chief Gunner's Mate
Joel E. Bean, Fireman 1st Class
Henry Wethley, Boatswain's Mate 1st class
Clarence J. Webster, Electrician 2nd Class
Fred G. Simcox, Quartermaster 3rd Class
Jay Williams, Ordinary Seaman

Included in the list of 71 names were awards to Lieutenant Victor Blue for "...locating the enemy's ships in Santiago Harbor, June 12, 1898" and Assistant Naval Constructor Richard P. Hobson, for "...sinking the *Merrimac* in entrance to Santiago Harbor, June 3, 1898."

A request for the engraving of 22 additional medals was contained in a letter to the U.S. Mint dated August 22, 1904:

US TORPEDO BOAT ERICSSON

Lieutenant Nathan R. Usher

Ensign John R. Edie

Ensign John J. Hannigan

Jacobus J. Corino, Chief Machinist

Clarence M. Wingate, Chief Machinist

David Hepburn, Chief Gunner's Mate

James H. Agnew, Fireman 1st Class

John Hill, Fireman 1st Class

Leonard Roll, Gunner's Mate 1st Class

Tanaka Shosuke, Ship's Cook 1st Class

Emile Van Castern, Quartermaster 1st Class

Daniel J. Hollingsworth, Gunner's Mate 2nd Class

Harry D. Rogers, Quartermaster 2nd Class

Alvah M. Smith, Gunner's Mate 2nd Class

Nicholas Calango, Water Tender

James K. Doherty, Oiler

John B. McNalley, Oiler

Shiroshi Otsuka, Cabin Steward

Robert H. Russell, Water Tender

James H.W. Centner, Seaman

Albert O. Maywald, Seaman

Maurice C. Minster, Seaman

There is also some correspondence indicating that this second request for the 22 medals was completed by the firm of Joseph K. Davison of Philadelphia. It is unclear whether the first 71 medals were actually engraved by the U.S. Mint. A possibility exists that there were differences in the wording and style of engraving between the first 71 and the later 22 medals.

There is also some unconfirmed evidence that additional awards were made as follows: Ensign Henry Ward, for "...obtaining valuable naval information within the lines of the enemy in Spain and Porto Rico, 1898;" Ensign William Henry Buck, for "...obtaining valuable information during the Spanish-American War, 1898;" Ensign Rochester Cuming, *USS Harvard*, for "rescue of crews;" Lieutenant Hilary Williams, *USS Iowa*, for "rescue of crews;" Gunner C.D. Holland, *USS Iowa*, for "rescue of crews;" Lieutenant Commander C.D. Bloch, for "rescue of crews;" John Bradshaw, *USS Harvard*, for "rescue of crews;" and to William J. Roberts (reason not stated). In 1910 the U.S. Mint was authorized to furnish a Specially Meritorious Service Medal to Maurice C. Minster, probably as a replacement for one which he had lost, since Minster previously received his medal for service on board the *USTB Ericsson*. An additional medal may have been awarded to Paymaster W.W. Galt for "Extraordinary heroism in bringing a launch from Kowloon to Mirs Bay the Raleigh's pump without which she could not have engaged in the battle of Manila Bay with both of her engines, April 26, 1898." No additional awards appear to have been made after 1912.

The designer of the Specially Meritorious Service Medal is unknown. The medal itself is a bronze cross pattee with a medallion in its center. In the center of the medallion is an anchor canted to the right and encircled by a wreath of oak and laurel. The wreath is encircled by an annulet bearing the inscription, *U.S. NAVAL CAMPAIGN WEST INDIES*. On the bottom arm of the cross is the date "1898;" on the left arm, the word, *SPECIALLY;* on the top arm, *MERITORIOUS;* and on the right arm, *SERVICE*. The reverse of the medal is blank, leaving space for the engraving of the recipient's name, rank, the deed performed, and the place and date of the act for which the medal was awarded. The ribbon is scarlet watered silk.

This little-known decoration is important because it became the precedent upon which later decorations for noncombat heroism were based.

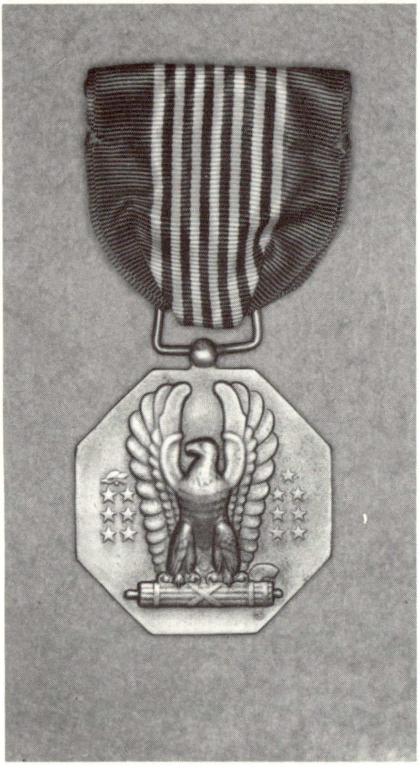

obverse

reverse

Soldier's Medal

THE SOLDIER'S MEDAL

(U.S. Army)

On numerous occasions over the years soldiers have performed noteworthy acts of heroism under noncombat circumstances. Such acts have included saving people from drowning, rescuing them from fires or other calamities, and feats of heroism rendered during natural disasters or accidents. Prior to its disestablishment in 1918, the Certificate of Merit could be awarded to an enlisted man for such heroism, although no comparable decoration existed for officers.

After the Certificate of Merit was disestablished there was no Army decoration at all for non-combat heroism. This deficiency was remedied when Congress authorized the Soldier's Medal on July 2, 1926. The Soldier's Medal is awarded to any member of the armed forces of the United States (or of a friendly foreign nation) who, while serving in any capacity with the United States Army, distinguishes himself by heroism not involving actual conflict with an armed enemy. The Soldier's Medal is comparable in standing to the Distinguished Flying Cross. To earn a Soldier's Medal, the act must have involved personal danger and the voluntary risk of one's life. This decoration is not awarded solely for saving a life, nor is there a requirement that a life be saved. The controlling feature of the Soldier's Medal is that to earn it, the recipient must engage in some heroic act involving personal risk. In the majority of cases, this happens to involve a life-saving effort.

The Soldier's Medal was designed by Gaetano Cecere. The medal itself is a bronze octagon one and three-eighths inches in circumscribing diameter. On the obverse it has an eagle displayed, standing on a fasces, between two groups of stars (one group has six stars and the other seven). Above the group of six stars is a crown of laurel. On the reverse is a shield paly of thirteen pieces; on the chief, the letters, "U.S." supported by sprays of laurel and oak. To the left of the spray of laurel (and along the edge of the medal) is the word, *SOLDIERS* and in the same position on the opposite side, *MEDAL*. Across the face are the words, *FOR VALOR*, above a plaque to be used for engraving the recipient's name. The medals were originally numbered on the bottom rim, but that practice has been discontinued since World War II.

The medal is suspended by a rectangular loop with rounded corners from a moired silk ribbon. The ribbon is composed of two outside stripes of blue; the center contains alternating stripes of white (seven) and red (six) of equal width.

The octagon shape was adopted to distinguish the Soldier's Medal from all other American decorations. The eagle is the American bald eagle, representing the United States. The fasces allude to the lawful authority of the State and symbolically signifies the fact that the medal is an award from the Government to the recipient. The stars allude to the original thirteen colonies and hence to the United States of America. The spray of laurel is used to make the groups of stars symmetrical and also represents the ancient symbol of achievement. On the reverse of the medal, the shield is from the Great Seal of the United States, and the sprays of laurel and oak allude to achievement and strength. The colors on the ribbon are the national colors, taken from the flag, the thirteen red and white stripes being arranged in the same manner (white alternating with red) as the thirteen vertical stripes of the shield of the United States Coat of Arms.

THE NAVY AND MARINE CORPS MEDAL

In 1941 the Chief of the Navy's Bureau of Navigation requested the Board of Awards to give consideration to the creation of two new decorations on the order of the Army's Soldier's Medal. He specifically sought a *Sailor's Medal* and a *Marine's Medal*, both to be awarded for non-combat heroism. He pointed out that "at the present time we depend on the Treasury Department to issue life saving medals. It is believed the Navy should be in a position to reward its own personnel without reference to other government departments." The Board approved the proposal on November 25, 1941.

In the meantime, draft legislation had been prepared for the creation of the "Sailor's Medal" and the "Marine's Medal," and was entered as HR 6275. On January 26, 1942, Secretary of the Navy Frank Knox wrote to the Chairman of the Committee on Naval Affairs (House of Representatives) stating that the Navy supported the proposed Bill providing that instead of the two medals, only one be authorized and that it be known as the "*Navy and Marine Corps Medal*." The Navy and Marine Corps Medal was thus established by Section 5 of Public Law #702, which was approved on August 7, 1942.

The Navy and Marine Corps Medal was authorized for award to any person who, while serving in any capacity with the United States Navy or Marine Corps, had, since December 6, 1941, distinguished himself or herself by heroism not involving actual conflict with an enemy. It was also authorized for award to any person who had received a letter of commendation for heroism from the Secretary of the Navy, regardless of the date of the act, provided that the recipient of the letter made application for the medal. The Navy and Marine Corps Medal is still awarded under essentially the same criteria. For acts of lifesaving, it is required that the action be performed at the risk of one's own life. It is not awarded solely on the basis of having saved a life, nor is the saving of a life an essential requirement for the medal.

The Navy and Marine Corps Medal was designed by Lieutenant Commander McClelland Barclay (who was lost in action off New Georgia Island during July of 1943). The medal is an octagonal shaped bronze medallion, in the center of which is an eagle facing to the left with upraised wings. The eagle is perched upon an anchor, and beneath the anchor is a globe. The legend, *HEROISM* appears at the base of the medal. The reverse of the medal is blank.

obverse

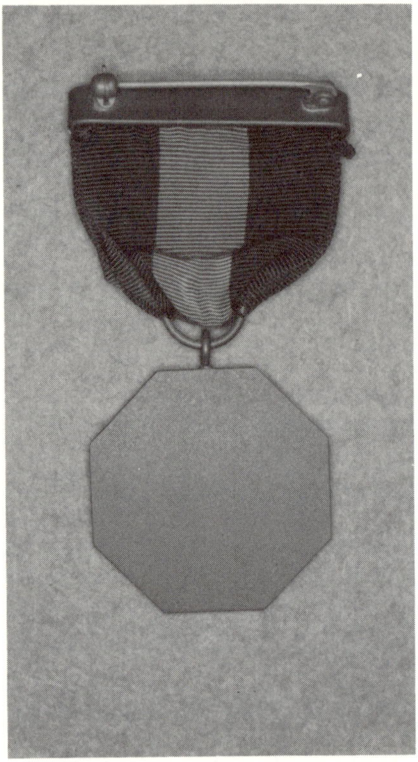

reverse

Navy & Marine Corps Medal

The shape of the medal follows the style set by the Soldier's Medal. The eagle is the American bald eagle and represents the United States. The anchor is used to indicate that the award is a naval decoration, and the globe is from the Marine Corps insignia and represents that service.

The ribbon, which was designed by M.A. Crawford, consists of equal sized stripes of navy blue, old gold, and scarlet, in that order. The blue and gold are the Navy's official colors and the scarlet and gold are the official colors of the U.S. Marine Corps.

Secretary of the Navy J. William Middendorf, II, presenting the Navy & Marine Corps Medal to Ensign Deborah Ann Burnette. The first woman to receive the Navy & Marine Corps Medal, Ensign Burnette rescued a child from the path of a speeding automobile. (US Navy photo)

obverse

reverse

Airman's Medal

THE AIRMAN'S MEDAL

(U.S. Air Force)

The Airman's Medal was established on July 6, 1960, by Public Law 86-593, which amended section 8750 of Title 10, United States Code, to provide the U.S. Air Force with a distinctive decoration in lieu of the Soldier's Medal. The Air Force had continued to use the Soldier's Medal after becomig a separate service, and the law which created the Soldier's Medal on July 2, 1926, was deemed to be the law which also authorized the Airman's Medal. The change in 1960 did not create a new decoration but merely authorized the Air Force to award its own version of the decoration which had been established when the Air Force was still a part of the Army.

The Airman's Medal is awarded to a person serving in any capacity with the U.S. Air Force for heroism involving voluntary risk of life under conditions other than those of conflict with an armed enemy of the United States. The saving of a life or the success of the voluntary heroic act is not essential.

The Airman's Medal was designed and sculpted by Thomas Hudson Jones of the Army's Institute of Heraldry. The medal is a bronze disc one and three-eighths inches in diameter with an oxidized satin finish. On the obverse of the medal is the figure of Hermes, son of Zeus, resting on one knee and releasing an eagle from his open hands. Directly in front of the figure of Hermes, who is in profile facing the viewer's left, and following the curvature of the medal, is the word, *AIRMAN'S* and in the same position behind the figure, *MEDAL*.

The reverse contains a stylized laurel wreath. Within the laurel wreath, and at the top of the medal in two lines, is the inscription, *FOR VALOR*. The ribbon is based on that of the Soldier's Medal; the alternating white and red stripes of the Soldier's Medal being replaced by alternating stripes of gold and blue (seven gold and six blue), bordered by stripes of pale blue.

The Airman's Medal is unique in that its shape does not follow the standard format of the other medals for non-combat heroism (octagonal), but is circular instead. The reason for this is that the design of the Airman's Medal was originally approved for use as the Air Force Distinguished Service Medal (all of the Distinguished Service Medals are round and both the Army and Navy DSM feature an eagle on the obverse). However, a more favored design for the USAF Distinguished Service Medal was subsequently submitted (and accepted), and since the first design had already been approved by the Commission on Fine Arts, it was decided to modify it for use as the Airman's Medal.

In terms of its symbolism, the Greek God Hermes, son of Zeus, represents youth, vigor, and boldness. The releasing of the eagle - the American bald eagle - alludes to the ideals and aspirations of American airmen. The laurel on the reverse alludes to achievement.

THE COAST GUARD MEDAL

The Coast Guard's search and rescue mission makes it inevitable that personnel of that service will occasionally be faced with extremely hazardous situations. After World War II, and in order to provide a parallel Coast Guard decoration to the Navy and Marine Corps Medal, the Coast Guard sought legislation which would allow it to present an appropriate counterpart decoration. Authority for the new decoration, known as the Coast Guard Medal, was accordingly granted by Act of Congress on August 4, 1949 (Title 14 U.S. Code, section 493).

The Coast Guard Medal is awarded to any person who, while serving in any capacity with the Coast Guard, distinguishes himself by heroism not involving actual combat with an enemy. To justify the Coast Guard Medal, the individual must have performed a voluntary act of heroism in the face of great danger. The act must have also extended beyond what would have normally been expected of the individual. For lifesaving, the individual must have displayed heroism at the risk of his life. The President has delegated authority to award the Coast Guard Medal to the Secretary of Transportation, who has further delegated the authority to the Commandant of the Coast Guard.

The Coast Guard Medal was designed and sculpted by Thomas Hudson Jones of the Army's Institute of Heraldry and is a bronze octagon. On its obverse it bears the Coast Guard Seal enclosed within a circle of continuous cable. The reverse is plain except for the inscription *FOR HEROISM* in raised letters. The ribbon is medium blue in the center and at the edges, with two sets of alternating white and red stripes (four white and three red).

Although the Coast Guard Medal was authorized in 1949, it was not designed and struck until 1958. It was first awarded in June of 1958. The first recipients were Engineman Third Class Earl A. Leyda and Boatswain's Mate Third Class Raymond A. Johnson, both of whom received the medal for their attempted rescue of workers trapped 5,800 feet below Lake Ontario after a tunnel explosion at Oswego, New York.

obverse

reverse

Coast Guard Medal

THE BRONZE STAR MEDAL

It became evident during the heavy fighting in the early campaigns of World War II that some type of junior decoration (comparable to the Air Medal for flight crews) was needed for ground and surface personnel. Although the Navy was interested in establishing a decoration to be known as the Bronze Star Medal, the War Department was opposed to the idea of creating any more new medals. However, General George C. Marshall provided the support needed to create the Bronze Star Medal. In a letter dated April 10, 1944, General Marshall wrote to Thomas W. Martin of the U.S. House of Representatives:

> I was so impressed with the effect of the Air Medal and for the long-suffering infantryman that I personally asked for and secured the President's approval to a corresponding decoration for the ground forces, to be known as the Bronze Star. I want to obtain the same effect with this among the ground troops, particularly the infantry who suffer such a high percentage of our casualties, and I intend that it shall be awarded with the same freedom as the Air Medal.

General Marshall wanted the front line troops to have an award which could be quickly conferred and which meant something to the soldier who earned it. Marshall went on to say, "I intend to see that these young soldiers enjoy this small fruit of their military effort while they are amongst their war comrades and confronted with the ordeal of further fighting."

General Marshall intended the Bronze Star Medal to be an award that could be used to "...sustain morale and fighting spirit in the face of continuous operations and severe losses." He had in mind the infantry rifleman, whose ranks suffered the heaviest casualties of all branches and who was forced to endure the greatest hardships. President Franklin D. Roosevelt concurred and created the Bronze Star Medal by Executive Order (EO 9419) on February 4, 1944.

The Bronze Star Medal is awarded to any person, who, while serving in any capacity with the Armed Forces of the United States after December 6, 1941, distinguishes himself by heroic or meritorious achievement or service (not involving participation in aerial flight) while engaged in an action against an enemy of the United States; while engaged in military operations involving conflict with an opposing foreign force; or, while serving with friendly foreign forces engaged in an armed conflict against an

obverse

reverse

Bronze Star Medal

opposing armed force in which the United States is not a belligerent party. In the case of heroism, awards may be made for acts performed under circumstances described above, but not of a character to warrant an award of the Silver Star. When the Bronze Star Medal is awarded for heroism, a bronze letter "V" is worn on the ribbon. Awards may also be made to recognize single acts of meritorious achievement or service. The required achievement or service, while of a lesser degree than that required for an award of the Legion of Merit, must nevertheless have been meritorious and accomplished with distinction.

The Bronze Star Medal was designed by Bailey, Banks and Biddle of Philadelphia and is a five-pointed star one and one-half inches in diameter from point to point. In the center of the star is a smaller star, three-sixteenths of an inch in circumscribing diameter, from which rays extend to the points of the outer star. On the reverse, in the center of the star, is an annulet of raised words, *HEROIC OR MERITORIOUS ACHIEVEMENT*, and within the words is a space for engraving the name or initials of the recipient. The ribbon is watered silk, predominantly red, with a stripe of blue in the center separated from the red by a narrow pinstripe of white. The ribbon is also edged in white.

The design of the Bronze Star Medal reflects the intent that it be a junior companion to the Silver Star. When the Commission on Fine Arts was presented with the proposed design of the Bronze Star it considered its similarity to the Silver Star and interposed no objections.

obverse

reverse

Defense Meritorious Service Medal

THE DEFENSE MERITORIOUS SERVICE MEDAL

The first decoration specifically intended for members of a joint service organization (as opposed to those assigned to a single service organization) was the Joint Service Commendation Medal, authorized in 1963. This was followed in 1970 by the creation of the Defense Distinguished Service Medal; in 1976 by the Defense Superior Service Medal (the Defense Department equivalent to the Legion of Merit); in 1977 by the Defense Meritorious Service Medal; and in 1983 by the Joint Service Achievement Medal. Thus, over time a set of decorations for meritorious achievement comparable to each of the noncombat decorations of the service branches was developed for award to individuals assigned to joint staffs, defense agencies, unified commands, or Department of Defense level assignments.

In a memorandum dated August 23, 1976, Major General Adrian St. John, who was at that time Vice Director of the Joint Staff of the Joints Chiefs of Staff, informed the Secretary of Defense that the Joint Chiefs of Staff had recommended the establishment of a Defense Meritorious Service Medal to "complete the joint decorations inventory." General St. John went on to say that the Joint Chiefs of Staff believed the establishment of a Defense Meritorious Service Medal would "serve as a means to recognize outstanding noncombat meritorious achievement or service for personnel assigned to the joint staffs or other joint activities of the Department of Defense."

Based on this recommendation, Vice Admiral John C. Finneran, who was then the Deputy Assistant Secretary of Defense, sent a memorandum on August 27, 1976, to the appropriate offices within the military departments soliciting their comments on the proposal. The replies were favorable, and on February 8, 1977, Admiral Finneran asked the Institute of Heraldry to prepare proposed designs for the medal. In June of 1977, a proposed Executive Order was sent to the White House for the President's approval, and on November 3, 1977, President Carter signed EO 12019, thereby officially establishing the Defense Meritorious Service Medal.

Meanwhile, the Institute of Heraldry had prepared four proposed designs for the medal. Major General Stanley Umstead, Jr., Deputy Assistant Secretary of Defense for Military Personnel Policy, selected design "D" and authorized the expenditure of $8000 for the development of tools, dies, and prototypes of the medal. On

November 15, 1977, the proposed design was submitted to the Commission of Fine Arts for its consideration, and the Commission granted its full approval on November 22, 1977.

The first samples of the new Defense Meritorious Service Medal were delivered to the Assistant Secretary of Defense for Manpower, Reserve Affairs and Logistics on July 5, 1978. The contract to produce the medals was awarded to His Lordship Products on February 21, 1979, and called for an initial order of 8,480 sets to be delivered by November of 1979.

The Defense Meritorious Service Medal is awarded to U.S military personnel assigned to any of the following joint activities: (1) the Office of the Secretary of Defense; (2) Washington Headquarters Services; (3) Organizations of the Joint Chiefs of Staff, joint activities reporting through the Joint Chiefs of Staff, and other agencies of the Joint Chiefs of Staff; (4) Defense agencies; (5) the Headquarters of Unified and Specified Commands; (6) Headquarters of joint forces, joint commands or control groups reporting to or through the Joint Chiefs of Staff, and headquarters of subordinate joint commands; (7) other joint activities reporting to Commanders of unified and specified commands such as Military Assistance Advisory Groups and Joint Missions; and (8) Jointly manned staffs within Allied Command Europe and Allied Command Atlantic, the NATO Military Committee, and military agencies associated with the functions of the military.

The Defense Meritorious Service Medal is awarded for noncombat meritorious achievement or service that is incontestably exceptional and of a magnitude that clearly places the individual above his peers while serving in one of the assignments for which a Defense Meritorious Service Medal has been designated (see preceeding paragraph).

The medal was designed by Mildred Orloff and sculpted by Lewis J. King, both of the Army Institute of Heraldry. It is a bronze medal one and one-half inches in diameter overall, consisting of a circular wreath of laurel tied with a ribbon at the base; in the center, a pentagon shape slightly overlapping the wreath; overall an eagle with wings upraised, standing at the base of the pentagon. On the reverse the medal bears the inscription *DEFENSE MERITORIOUS SERVICE* in three horizontal lines; and around the bottom, the words, *UNITED STATES OF AMERICA*. In terms of its symbolism, the eagle represents the United States, the pentagon alludes to the Department of Defense, and the laurel wreath represents achievement. The ribbon consists of vertical stripes of white, red, and blue.

THE MERITORIOUS SERVICE MEDAL

On February 11, 1919, General John J. Pershing wrote that he was "...desirous of issuing a Meritorious Service Medal, or a medal to be known by some other appropriate name, that may be presented for acts or services that are worthy of recommendation but do not come within the requirements for the presentation of the Distinguished Service Medal or the Distinguished Service Cross." On February 17, 1919, the Judge Advocate General of the Army stated that he was of the opinion the President could authorize the Meritorious Service Medal as a part of the uniform. However, by that time the "Great War For Civilization" had ended three months earlier, and the issue of new medals no longer seemed important. General Pershing's request fell on deaf ears and was disapproved.

During World War II a substantial number of new decorations were approved to fill specific needs, but the idea of establishing a Meritorious Service Medal for military personnel was not raised. It was not until after World War II that the need for a Meritorious Service Medal was again brought to light. In 1948 the idea was studied but apparently did not receive serious consideration. In 1956, the U.S. Air Force conducted a study of decorations to replace those which it had carried over from the days when it was part of the Army, and their proposal included the recommendation for a Meritorious Service Medal (which at that time they called the "Air Force Achievement Medal"). The Air Force study noted that there was a tremendous gap between the Legion of Merit and the Commendation Medal. They pointed out that in wartime this gap was filled by the Bronze Star, but there was no peacetime decoration comparable to the Bronze Star. The Air Force specifically recommended that the Meritorious Service Medal be created and that it be used to recognize military members for "exceptionally meritorious performance of distinctive service of other than national or international significance." The proposal did not meet with success and the push for a Meritorious Service Medal was again dropped.

The issue was raised again during the Vietnam War. In 1969 Vice Admiral William E. Gentner (Ret), who was then Chief of the Navy Board of Decorations and Medals, argued that a Meritorious Service Medal would "do a great deal to establish a continuity in non-combat awards by maintaining the Legion of Merit in a selective category, and at the same time, keep the Service Commendation Medal in the area for which it was conceived."

obverse

reverse

Meritorious Service Medal

There was yet another reason that the creation of a Meritorious Service Medal was seen as desirable. The Bronze Star Medal had been liberally awarded in Vietnam, especially for "meritorious service," and this was seen as diluting its value as a decoration for heroism. The idea of a Meritorious Service Medal, which would be a non-combat decoration on a par with the Bronze Star Medal, appealed to those who were concerned about the declining value of the Bronze Star Medal.

The service branches agreed to the desirability of establishing the Meritorious Service Medal and the necessary staff work was completed. As one of his last acts as President of the United States, Lyndon B. Johnson signed Executive Order 11448 on January 16, 1969, creating the Meritorious Service Medal.

The Meritorious Service Medal may be awarded to any member of the Armed Forces of the United States who distinguishes himself by either outstanding achievement or meritorious service to the United States. To justify this decoration according to Navy policy, the acts or services rendered by an individual, regardless of grade, must have been comparable to that required for the Legion of Merit but in a duty of lesser responsibility. According to Army and Air Force policy, the act or achievement need not be the same as would be required for an award of the Legion of Merit. For all service branches the Meritorious Service Medal is the counterpart of the Bronze Star Medal for the recognition of meritorious noncombat service. When the degree of meritorious achievement or service rendered is not sufficient to warrant the award of the Meritorious Service Medal, the Commendation Medal (when appropriate) is normally considered.

The Meritorious Service Medal was designed by Jay Morris and sculpted by Lewis J. King, Jr., both of the Army's Institute of Heraldry. It is a bronze medal one and one-half inches in diameter overall, consisting of six rays issuant from the upper three points of a five-pointed star with bevelled edges and containing two smaller stars defined by incised outlines; in front of the lower part of the star is an eagle with wings upraised, standing upon two upward curving branches of laurel tied with a ribbon between the feet of the eagle. The reverse is plain except for a circular inscription in raised letters which says, *UNITED STATES OF AMERICA* in the upper half and *MERITORIOUS SERVICE* in the lower half. The two halves are separated by raised dots. The ribbon is composed of a central stripe of ruby bordered on both sides by a stripe of white and edged with a stripe of ruby.

In terms of its symbolism, the eagle represents the nation and the laurel branches denote achievement. The star is used to represent the military service and the rays emanating therefrom denote the constant efforts of individuals to achieve through excellent and meritorious service.

General John J. Pershing (in an oil portrait by Bertie Poston). General Pershing was the first to recommend a "Meritorious Service Medal" -- but it took 51 years for it to become a reality. (US Army photo)

THE AIR MEDAL

On March 9, 1942, Secretary of War Henry L. Stimson sent a proposed Executive Order to the Director of the Bureau of the Budget. The Executive Order called for the creation of a decoration to be known as the *Air Medal*. Stimson pointed out that the Distinguished Flying Cross was available only for heroism or extraordinary achievement in aerial flight, but that he "...desired to have available for morale purposes a decoration with less stringent qualifications...." He went on to note that the new and unusual flight duties "...now being performed by the Air Force Combat Command and the Air Force Ferrying Command illustrate the need for such an award." In a separate letter dated April 13, 1942, Secretary of the Navy James Forrestal concurred with Stimson's recommendation. The package was forwarded to the President, who scribbled "approved" on the bottom, which he signed as "C in C." The formal Executive Order (EO 9158) was signed on May 11, 1942. The Air Medal has been subject to frequent criticism because of the large numbers which have been awarded. For example, during World War II, 1,166,471 Air Medals were awarded by the Army alone, accounting for 65% of all Army decorations awarded during World War II. Of this total, 341,507 were original awards and 824,964 were oak leaf clusters. However, as General George C. Marshall pointed out in April of 1944:

> The air decoration should be measured against the remarkable achievements of the Air Forces and the special nature of continuing combat. For example, at the end of 1943 the Army Air Forces had flown 392,000 combat sorties, exposing 1,375,000 individuals to the danger of enemy fire. They have lost their hands and their feet in flying and fighting at temperatures far below zero. They suffered heavy loss of pilots or crew members, and almost as many sorties have been flown in the past three months of 1944 as in all of 1943.
>
> These are the men who pioneered the daylight bombing over Europe when the usual pessimistic predictions were that such tactics would be suicidal. They are the men who fought the Japanese air force against tremendous odds until they ultimately gained air superiority. They continued to fly missions when their chance of safe return was apparently less than one in five. They still take heavy casualties day after day, week after week. Yet their morale has continued high and their achievements have soared, and one of the reasons is that they receive positive evidence that their work has been given immediate recognition through awards of the Air Medal.

obverse

reverse

Air Medal

The Air Medal was made retroactive to September 8, 1939, the date of the limited national emergency proclaimed by President Roosevelt (based on the outbreak of war in Europe). It is awarded to any member of the Armed Forces of the United States for heroic or meritorious achievement while participating in aerial flight. Although the requirements are less than that required for award of the Distinguished Flying Cross, they must nevertheless be accomplished with distinction above and beyond what would normally be expected. Despite the fact that each branch of the Armed Forces sets its own specific criteria for awarding the Air Medal, all are similar. In general, the Air Medal may be awarded for acts of heroism in connection with military operations against an armed enemy or while engaged in military operations involving conflict with an opposing armed force in which the United States is not a belligerent party, which are of a lesser degree than required for award of the Distinguished Flying Cross. The Air Medal may also be awarded for non-combat aerial achievement, as it is for example, to air weather crews who gather data on tornadoes by flying into them.

The Air Medal may also be awarded for single acts of outstanding achievement which involve superior airmanship but of a lesser degree than would justify an award of a Distinguished Flying Cross. Finally, awards for meritorious service may be made for sustained distinction in the performance of duties involving regular and frequent participation in aerial flight operations. These operations include "strikes" (sorties which deliver ordnance against the enemy; those which land or evacuate personnel in an assault; or, those which involve search and rescue operations which encounter enemy opposition); "flights" (sorties which involve the same kinds of operations as strikes but which do not encounter enemy opposition); or "Direct Combat Support" (sorties which include such activies as reconnaissance, target combat air patrol, electronics countermeasures support, psychological warfare, coastal surveillance, and so on).

The Air Medal was designed by Walker K. Hancock who, in an open competition, won $1,500 for his design (shortly after he learned that his design had been selected, the forty-one year old artist was drafted into the Army!). The medal is a bronze compass rose of sixteen points surmounted by a fleur-de-lis. In the center of the obverse is an eagle swooping downward, clutching a lightning bolt in each talon. The reverse has a raised table for inscribing the recipient's name but is otherwise blank. The ribbon is a broad stripe of ultramarine blue in the center, bordered on each side by a stripe of golden orange and edged in ultramarine blue.

The symbolism of the Air Medal is simple and direct: the compass rose indicates the global capacity of American air might, represented by the American bald eagle. The lightning bolts in the eagle's talons allude to the strength of the United States and its ability to wage unlimited war. The fleur-de-lis, the French symbol of nobility, alludes to the high ideals of American airmen. The colors of the ribbon were selected because they were the colors of the Army Air Corps.

THE JOINT SERVICE COMMENDATION MEDAL

On March 26, 1963, General Maxwell D. Taylor, who was then Chairman of the Joint Chiefs of Staff, sent a memorandum to the Secretary of Defense concerning "recognition of outstanding service with joint activities." General Taylor pointed out that "during recent years the establishment of unified and specified commands and other joint agencies has increased the number of personnel assigned to joint activities." He noted that several of the commanders of unified commands had expressed a need for some means by which they could recognize outstanding service or meritorious achievement by individuals assigned to the headquarters of those commands.

General Taylor proposed the establishment of a Joint Service Commendation Medal as a solution to this problem. General Taylor's memorandum was clear as to what kinds of organizations would be eligible to award the medal and was equally clear as to those which could not. The latter category included such agencies as the Atomic Energy Commission, the Federal Aviation Administration, the National Aeronautics and Space Administration, the Selective Service System, the Central Intelligence Agency, and the State Department. General Taylor pointed out that "...If we broaden the lease to include such agencies ... we would then have to include all agencies ... which have military personnel assigned outside their respective service." Taylor felt that such a broad inclusion violated the intent of a Joint Service Commendation Medal, which he envisioned as being used only by joint or unified military organizations composed of members of the various service branches.

General Taylor's recommendation was accepted and the Joint Service Commendation Medal was established under the authority of the Secretary of Defense on June 25, 1963, by Department of Defense Directive 1348.14. The Joint Service Commendation Medal is awarded to any member of the armed forces of the United States serving in an assignment in any of a variety of joint activities, such as with the Office of the Secretary of Defense; the Joint Chiefs of Staff; the National Security Agency; or Defense Department agencies or joint activities which report through the Joint Chiefs of Staff, and so on.

obverse

reverse

Joint Service Commendation Medal

The Joint Service Commendation Medal may be awarded for either outstanding achievement or meritorious service. Although the achievement or service may be less than that required for award of the Defense Meritorious Service Medal, it must nevertheless be accomplished with distinction. It takes precedence with, but is worn before, the commendation medals of the separate services.

General Maxwell D. Taylor. General Taylor proposed the creation of the Joint Service Commendation Medal to reward outstanding service to military members assigned to joint commands. (US Army photo)

The medal was designed by Stanford F. Potter of the Institute of Heraldry. The obverse consists of four green enameled hexagons which are conjoined, two vertically and two horizontally. In the center of the medal is an eagle with shield and three arrows in its talons. Above the eagle is a field of thirteen stars, and beneath it is a stylized heraldic delineation. The entire medal is surmounted by a circular wreath in gold which is bound with gold bands. The reverse has a table in the center, and above the table are the words, *FOR MILITARY* in two rows, and below the tablet, the word,*MERIT*. At the base of the reverse is a stylized spray of laurel. The ribbon is the standard size and consists of a center stripe of green bordered by stripes of white, green, white, and blue.

In terms of its symbolism, the four hexagons represent the Army, Navy, Air Force and Marine Corps (their respective commendation medals all have hexagonal shapes). The fact that the hexagons are conjoined suggests both the individuality of each of the service branches along with the unity of joint service. The stylized delineation represents the primary theaters of the service branches: land, air and sea. The eagle, shield, arrows and thirteen stars are taken from the seal of the Secretary of Defense, under whose authority the medal is granted. The laurel wreath signifies achievement, and the green enamel represents faithfulness and unity.

Assistant to the Secretary of Defense for Legislative Affairs David E. McGiffert makes first presentation of the Joint Service Commendation Medal (to Lt Col Bruce F. Meyers), July 1963.

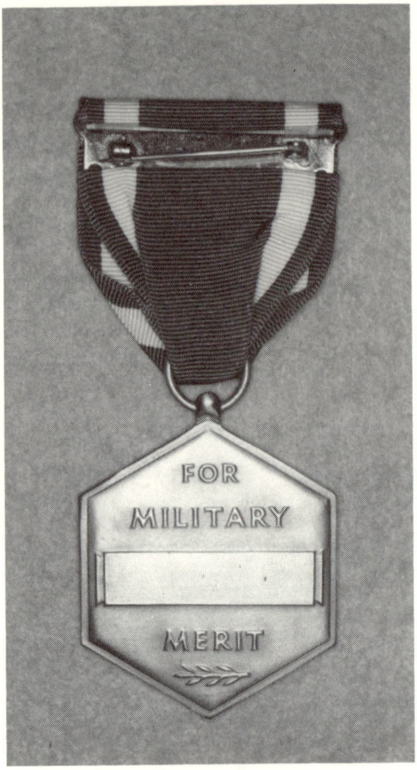

obverse

reverse

Navy Commendation Medal

THE NAVY COMMENDATION MEDAL

In 1943 it became apparent to Navy officials that some "junior visible recognition for surface forces comparable to the Air Medal for flight personnel" was needed. The establishment of a new decoration - the Bronze Star - was discussed with the War Department, but at that time the War Department was against the establishment of any more medals.

In September of 1943, the Commander in Chief, U.S. Pacific Fleet (in a letter on the general subject of medals and awards), recommended that a ribbon be authorized to be worn by recipients of letters of commendation by Fleet Commanders or higher authority and that no medal was to be involved. The Commander in Chief, U.S. Fleet, concurred but recommended that it be limited to commendations from the Secretary of the Navy or the Commander in Chief of a Fleet. The Navy Board of Decorations and Medals, after studying the subject, submitted the following recommendation to the Secretary of the Navy: "That a ribbon to be known as *Commendation Ribbon* be authorized to be worn by the recipients of Letters of Commendation from the Secretary of the Navy or Commanders in Chief of a Fleet issued subsequent to 6 December 1941 for meritorious service or heroism and that the authorization to wear the Commendation Ribbon be included in the text of the commendation for such letters as are addressed after the date of promulgation of the governing orders, if the issuing officer desires that it carry this privilege." The Secretary of the Navy approved the Board's recommendation on November 1, 1943, and on January 11, 1944, issued ALNAV #11 establishing the Commendation Ribbon. It is not known whether or not the Secretary of the Navy consulted with the President on the subject. Interestingly enough, shortly after the Commendation Ribbon was officially authorized, the War Department reversed its previous stand on the Bronze Star Medal and asked the Navy's concurrence in seeking the President's approval for its creation. The Navy concurred, and the Bronze Star Medal was established by Executive Order 9419 on February 4, 1944. If the Bronze Star had been in existence prior to the establishment of the Commendation Ribbon, it is very unlikely that the Commendation Ribbon would have been established. However, the Navy felt that "...it was not considered conducive to good morale to withdraw it. Moreover, the ribbon still answers a very useful purpose in recognizing certain types of acts or services for which the Bronze Star Medal cannot be awarded."

After the Second World War there was periodic interest in the creation of a medal to accompany the Commendation Ribbon. On September 26, 1946, in a letter from the Navy Board of Decorations and Medals to the Secretary of the Navy, the Board stated that it felt that creating a medal for the "Secretary's Commendation Ribbon was unnecessary and undesirable because the original reason for the commendation was to recognize minor acts or services of a commendatory nature not sufficiently meritorious to justify a decoration. The purpose for which the ribbon was specifically established would, therefore, be annulled." This position clearly reflected the belief that the Commendation Ribbon was not a decoration and that no medal (which by its very nature would have been a decoration) should be created to accompany the Commendation Ribbon.

Approximately three years later, on July 20, 1949, Army Circular 91/Air Force Letter 35-25 announced a "metal pendant" for their Commendation Ribbon. In November of 1949, the National President of the Marine Corps Reserve Officers Association wrote to the Commandant of the Marine Corps recommending that "...in light of unification policies, the Navy Department establish a metal pendant for the Navy Commendation Ribbon similar or identical to that authorized by the Army and Air Force." The Commandant agreed, and in a letter dated November 23, 1949, to the Secretary of the Navy he recommended that the "metal pendant" be adopted, in spite of the fact that the Board of Decorations and Medals was of the opinion that "...the issuance of a metal pendant to holders of the Commendation Ribbon would lessen the personal value of medals presented to holders of higher awards." However, the Chief of Naval Operations concurred with the suggestion that the Navy Department establish a "...metal pendant similar or identical to that of the Army and Air Force."

Acting on the recommendation of the Chief of Naval Operations, the Board of Decorations and Medals issued a report on February 15, 1950, in which they said that, "After a careful review of the advantages and disadvantages of the basic proposal, the Board recommends, in view of its importance to good public relations, that the Navy Department establish the metal pendant for the Navy Commendation Ribbon." However, the Board was clear on two points: that it not be considered a decoration and that the name *metal pendant* not be changed to *commendation medal.* Finally, the Board suggested that the Navy adopt the design of the metal pendant to be used by the Army and the Air Force, except that it use the ribbon which had been in use for the Navy

Commendation Ribbon. On March 20, 1950, the Secretary of the Navy approved the recommendation, and on April 6, 1950, the Navy announced the establishment of the metal pendant to accompany the Navy Commendation Ribbon. On July 8, 1960, the Chief of Naval Operations wrote to the Secretary of the Navy and requested that the name be changed from *Commendation Ribbon with Metal Pendant* to *Navy Commendation Medal*. On August 11, 1960, the Secretary of the Navy agreed, and the award was accordingly redesignated as the Navy Commendation Medal on September 21, 1960.

The Navy Commendation Medal is considered to be a decoration and is awarded to any person who, while serving in any capacity with the Navy or Marine Corps (including foreign military personnel and members of U.S. reserve components on active or inactive duty), distinguishes himself after December 6, 1941, by heroism, outstanding achievement or meritorious service. To merit this decoration, the act or service must be accomplished or performed in a manner above that normally expected and must be sufficient to distinguish the individual above those performing similar acts or services.

The medal itself was designed by Thomas Hudson Jones of the Army's Institute of Heraldry (originally for the Army and Air Force). It is a one and three-eighths inch bronze hexagon, one point up. In the center of the obverse is an American bald eagle with wings displayed horizontally, grasping three crossed arrows and bearing on its breast a shield paly of thirteen pieces and a chief. On the reverse, there is a blank plaque in the center (for inscribing the recipient's name). Above the plaque are the words, *FOR MILITARY* and below it, the word *MERIT*. There is a spray of laurel below the word *MERIT*. The ribbon is myrtle green with a white stripe toward either edge.

The shape of the medal was designed to distinguish it from all other decorations. The eagle is from the seal of the Department of Defense, and the shield on the eagle's breast is taken from the Great Seal of the United States. The laurel spray on the reverse is symbolic of achievement.

obverse

reverse

Army Commendation Medal

THE ARMY COMMENDATION MEDAL

Following the example set by the Navy, on December 18, 1945, the Secretary of War issued War Department Circular 377 which established the Army Commendation Ribbon. The Army Commendaton Ribbon did not have an accompanying medal and was intended for award to any person serving with the Army who, on or after December 7, 1941, distinguished himself either in combat or by meritorious achievement or service. In addition, any person who had received a letter of commendation signed by a Major General or higher for meritorious achievement or service conducted on or after December 7, 1941, could, upon application, receive an Army Commendation Ribbon.

Army Circular 91 (Air Force Letter 35-25) of July 20, 1949, announced a metal pendant for the Commendation Ribbon. For a while the award was known as the *Commendation Ribbon with Metal Pendant*, but was subsequently changed to the *Army Commendation Medal*. The Army Commendation Medal is awarded to any member of the Armed Forces of the United States who, while serving in any capacity with the Army on or after December 7, 1941, distinguishes himself by an act of heroism, extraordinary achievement, or meritorious service which has been of mutual benefit to a friendly nation and the United States.

Awards may be made for acts of valor performed under circumstances described above which are of lesser degree than required for award of the Bronze Star Medal. These acts may involve aerial flight. An award may be made for acts of non-combat heroism which do not meet the requirements for an award of the Soldier's Medal. When awarded for outstanding achievement or meritorious service, the act or service to be rewarded must be less than that required for award of a Meritorious Service Medal but more than that required for an Army Achievement Medal. The Army Commendation Medal may not be awarded to general officers.

The Army Commendation Medal was designed by Thomas Hudson Jones of the Army's Institute of Heraldry. It is a one and three-eighths inch bronze hexagon, one point up. In the center of the obverse is an American bald eagle with wings displayed horizontally, grasping three crossed arrows and bearing on its breast a shield paly of thirteen pieces and a chief. On the reverse, there is a blank plaque in the enter (for inscribing the recipient's name). Above the plaque are the words, *FOR MILITARY* and below it, *MERIT*. There is a spray of laurel below the word *MERIT*. The ribbon is the same shade of green as the ribbon to the Navy Commendation Medal. It is edged in white and contains five white pinstripes in the center.

The shape of the medal was designed to distinguish the Commendation Medal from all other decorations and has subsequently been used as the shape for the commendation medals of the other services. The eagle is taken from the seal of the Department of Defense, and the shield on the eagle's breast is taken from the Great Seal of the United States. The laurel spray on the reverse is symbolic of achievement.

THE AIR FORCE COMMENDATION MEDAL

After its establishment as a separate service, the Air Force continued to use the same Commendation Medal issued by the Army. This changed on March 24, 1958, when the Secretary of the Air Force established the Air Force Commendation Medal as a separate decoration. Its award to Air Force personnel was announced on March 28, 1958, in Air Force General Order Number 16.

The Air Force Commendation Medal is awarded for outstanding achievement or meritorious service rendered specifically on behalf of the Air Force, but not of such a nature as to merit award of the Meritorious Service Medal -- but more than would be required for award of the Air Force Achievement Medal. It is also awarded for acts of courage that do not meet the requirements of the Airman's Medal. The Air Force Commendation Medal may also be awarded for sustained meritorious performance by crew members, but may not be awarded to an officer who holds the rank of general.

The Air Force Commendation Medal was designed by Thomas Hudson Jones of the Army's Institute of Heraldry. The medal itself is a bronze hexagon one point up and is one and three-eighths inches wide, finished in a light brown patina. In the center of the medal on its obverse is the coat of arms of the Department of the Air Force. Above the coat of arms is an eagle with its wings extended, and behind the eagle is a cloud formation. The reverse contains a plaque for the recipient's name. Above the plaque, in three lines, are the words *FOR MILITARY MERIT* in raised letters, with the word *MILITARY* arched. The ribbon is moired silk composed primarily of yellow with Air Force Blue edges and three bands of Air Force blue spaced in the center.

The Air Force coat of arms gives high symbolic importance to the design and marks it as an Air Force decoration. The eagle is the American bald eagle and represents the nation. The cloud formation behind the eagle depicts the creation of a new firmament.

obverse

reverse

USAF Commendation Medal

THE COAST GUARD COMMENDATION MEDAL

Following the lead of first the Navy and then the Army and Air Force, the Secretary of the Treasury (under which the Coast Guard then operated) established the "Coast Guard Commendation Ribbon with Metal Pendant" on August 26, 1947. This award was to be granted "to members of the Armed Forces of the United States, serving in any capacity with the Coast Guard, for meritorious service resulting in unusual and outstanding achievement rendered while the Coast Guard is serving under Treasury Department jurisdiction." On October 2, 1959, it was redesignated as the *Coast Guard Commendation Medal* by order of the Commandant of the Coast Guard.

To merit this decoration, the outstanding achievement or meritorious service must have been accomplished in a manner above that which would have normally been expected and must be sufficient to distinguish the individual from those of comparable grade or rating performing similar acts or services. The heroism, outstanding achievement or meritorious service must be worthy of special recognition, but not of a level which would justify a Bronze Star Medal, Meritorious Service Medal, or an Air Medal yet more than would be required for award of the Coast Guard Achievement Medal.

The Coast Guard Commendation Medal has gone through two designs (both executed by the Army's Institute of Heraldry). The first was designed and sculpted by Frank Gasparro. The second version was designed by Jay Morris and sculpted by Lewis J. King, Jr. The first design was employed while the Coast Guard was under the jurisdiction of the Treasury Department and the second was adopted when it was placed under the Department of Transportation.

The first design is a bronze hexagon, point up. In the center of the obverse is the former Coast Guard Seal which embodied elements of the Treasury Department Seal, the whole being encircled by a continuous cable. There is a blank plaque in the center of the reverse, and the plaque is encircled by a laurel wreath. Above the plaque, in two lines, are the words *FOR OUTSTANDING* and below it, the word *SERVICE*. The plaque, words, and wreath are encircled by a continuous cable.

The second design, which was approved by the Commandant on June 11, 1968, is very similar to the first and also employs a bronze hexagon, point up. In the center of the obverse is the current Coast Guard Seal. The continuous cable used in the first design is deleted from the second. The reverse contains an

obverse

reverse

USCG Commendation Medal
(1947 - 1968)

annulet consisting of the word *AWARDED* at the top and, separated by stylized laurel leaves, the words *OUTSTANDING SERVICE* in the bottom. In the center are the words *TO* and *FOR*, separated by space for engraving the recipient's name. The ribbon for both designs is the same and is identical to that of the Navy Commendation Medal except for the addition of a narrow pin-stripe of white in the center of the ribbon.

obverse

reverse

USCG Commendation Medal
(1968 - present)

obverse

reverse

Joint Service Achievement Medal

THE JOINT SERVICE ACHIEVEMENT MEDAL

On March 11, 1982, Lt General William J. Hilsman, Director of the Defense Communications Agency, sent a memorandum on the subject of "joint awards" to Lt General R. Dean Tice, the Deputy Assistant Secretary of Defense (Military Personnel and Force Management), in which he recommended the establishment of an achievement medal to rank with the service achievement medals. General Hilsman specifically wanted a decoration which would complete the Department of Defense awards hierarchy and thereby provide a system of decorations for meritorious achievement comparable to those of the separate services. The establishment of such a medal, he believed, would also protect the integrity of the more senior Joint Service Commendation Medal and would negate any connotation that being assigned to a joint activity would be likely to result in decreased opportunity to earn recognition.

General Hilsman's proposal was coordinated with the Military Services for their comments. Although there was generally strong support by the separate services for the proposal, the resulting study noted that the number of individuals who would be eligible for the award would be small and those who became eligible could be adequately recognized by receiving the Achievement Medal of their respective service. Part of the problem was that because of their level of responsibility, most individuals who distinguished themselves while assigned to a joint activity should normally be eligible for either the Joint Service Commendation Medal or the Defense Meritorious Service Medal, thus making an achievement medal unnecessary.

Based on the foregoing, on August 30, 1982, Assistant Secretary of Defense Lawrence J. Korb sent a memorandum to the appropriate Assistant Secretaries of the Army, Navy, and Air Force informing them that, "...after consideration of all comments, the development of a Defense Achievement Medal is not warranted." He went on to say that, "...members assigned to organizations that qualify them for joint awards can be adequately recognized with Military Department awards and organizational certificates if the Joint Service Commendation Medal or higher award is not warranted." Finally, Korb stated that, "...each department must develop policy permitting recognition of their members jointly assigned and members from their sister services, if not currently established. This is to include individuals assigned to joint activities for which your department has been established as the executive agent." Thus, it would seem, the issue of a Defense Achievement Medal had come to a dead end.

Several months later, on March 10, 1983, Admiral Robert J. Long (Commander, CINCPAC), sent a message to General Tice in which he raised several problems with the policy previously articulated by Korb. In a nutshell, he was not satisfied and wanted the matter of a Defense Achievement Medal re-examined. On May 9, 1983, General Tice sent a memorandum to the appropriate Assistant Secretaries of the Army, Navy, and Air Force as well as to the Director of the Joint Staff (Joint Chiefs of Staff). In this memo, General Tice pointed out that, "Several months ago we indicated that a Joint Service Achievement Medal was not warranted in response to a Defense Communications Agency memorandum. We suggested several actions to you to make the utilization of service Achievement Medals feasible. This has not worked to the benefit of our jointly assigned people." General Tice went on to say, "I believe now is the time to develop a Joint Service Achievement Medal."

Tice requested that each of the services furnish their recommendations by June 22, 1983, and all of them did so, concurring with the proposal. On July 7, 1983, the Assistant General Counsel (Manpower and Health Affairs) pointed out that since the proposed Joint Service Achievement Medal would rank as the least prestigious DoD sponsored medal for joint duty, it should most properly be established by DoD directive. Accordingly, on August 1, 1983, a memorandum was prepared for Secretary of Defense Caspar Weinberger recommending he establish the Joint Service Achievement Medal. On August 3, 1983, Secretary Weinberger signed his approval to the memorandum, thus creating the decoration and establishing the earliest date of eligibility for its award.

Following Secretary Weinberger's approval, the administrative procedures necessary to bring the medal into physical reality began. The Assistant Secretary of Defense (Comptroller) was asked on August 9, 1983, to provide a fund citation authorizing approximately $15,000 to develop and procure the medal, and on the same date, the Institute of Heraldry was tasked with responsibility for preparing suggested designs. On December 7, 1983, a proposed Department of Defense Directive establishing eligibility criteria as well as award procedures was forwarded to all conerned agencies and offices along with instructions to return their comments by February 10, 1984. On January 31, 1984, the proposed design for the medal was approved by the Commission on Fine Arts.

The Joint Service Achievement Medal is awarded under the authority of Section 133 of Title 10, U.S. Code, and is implemented by Department of Defense Directive 1348. The medal is awarded in the name of the Secretary of Defense for either outstanding achievement or meritorious service and takes precedence before the Achievement Medals of the Military Services. It may not be awarded to any service member for an act or a period of service for which an Achievement Medal of a Military Service is awarded, nor may it be awarded for retirement. To be eligible for a Joint Service Achievement Medal, the individual must be a member of the Armed Forces of the United States and must be below the grade of O-6. He or she must be assigned to a qualifying organization (such as the Office of the Secretary of Defense, the Office of the Joints Chiefs of Staff, the Defense Agencies, Headquarters of Unified Commands, etc). The required achievement or service, while of lesser degree than that required for award of the Joint Service Commendation Medal, must have been accomplished with distinction.

The medal was designed by Jay Morris and sculpted by Donald Borja, both of the Institute of Heraldry. It is officially described as "a bronze medal 1-7/16 inches in diameter overall consisting of a star of twelve points and superimposed thereon an eagle holding three arrows as adapted from the seal of the Department of Defense." The reverse is plain except for a circle consisting of the words *JOINT SERVICE ACHIEVEMENT AWARD.* The ribbon contains a center stripe of red flanked on either side by stripes of light blue, white, green, white, and blue.

In terms of its symbolism, the eagle holding three arrows suggests the nation's readiness to defend in the air, on land and at sea. The raised points of the star denote vigilance in all directions.

obverse

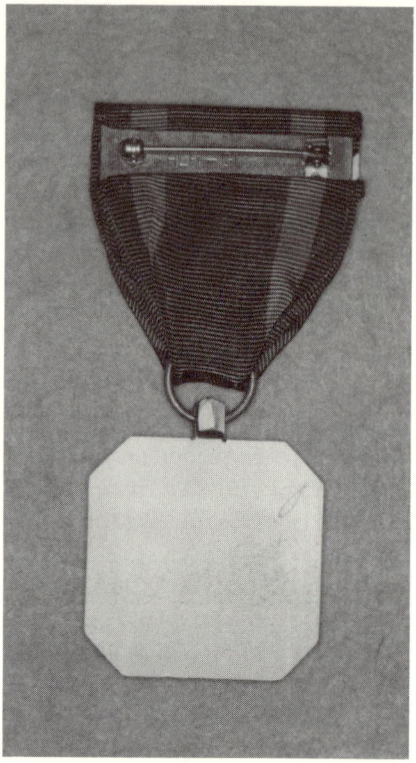

reverse

Navy Achievement Medal

THE NAVY ACHIEVEMENT MEDAL

On April 18, 1961, Secretary of the Navy John B. Connally wrote a letter to the Undersecretary of the Navy concerning his desire to create some form of recognition for outstanding leadership or contributions made by junior personnel of the Navy. Connally believed that junior officers and enlisted personnel who give their job more than is required, and in the process make an important or lasting contribution, should be entitled to recognition more tangible (and less private) than was possible through a routine fitness report. Connally also wanted to stimulate the pursuit of excellence and improvement, particularly in the fields of operations, administration, and management. He was especially interested in establishing an award which would recognize individuals in (or below) the rank of lieutenant commander in the Navy or major in the Marine Corps who excell in the performance of their duties or who make an outstanding contribution. Connally sought comments on how his objective could best be achieved and noted that he wanted to implement the award on or before May 1, 1961.

The Marine Corps, in a memo dated April 24, 1961, (responding to Secretary Connally's letter) was against the idea of creating a new award and suggested that existing awards be better utilized. However, the Chief of Naval Operations, in his letter of April 26, 1961, had mixed feelings. He said that "*...a substantial increase in the use of an existing award tends to reduce the distinction accorded to previous recipients,*" but went on to note that "*...a large number of personnel appear to believe that dedicated performance should be encouraged by other than an award or prize system.*" In spite of these misgivings, the Chief of Naval Operations went on to recommend the establishment of a "SECNAV Commendation for Achievement" to be awarded in recognition of exceptional achievement in the fields of operations, administration, and management. The Chief of Naval Operations also believed that "...exemplary performance in the overall field of leadership, but based on specific achievement" should also be a criterion. He recommended that the award take the form of a formal citation and ribbon, but that no medal be created to go with the ribbon.

Secretary Connally accepted the recommendation, and on May 1, 1961, SECNAV Instruction 1650.16 was issued establishing the Secretary of the Navy Commendation for Achievement Award with Ribbon. The ribbon was to consist of a background of Irish green with two stripes of Indian orange toward either edge. Because the award was created rather quickly, certain problems arose including "the unwieldiness of the title, delegation of authority, whether it would be used only for peacetime achievements, etc." In April of 1962 the title of the award was shortened to "SECNAV Commendation for Achievement" and the other problem areas were addressed by personnel officers.

On November 18, 1963, the Bureau of Personnel prepared a memorandum raising the question of how the SECNAV Commendation for Achievement was to be worn when full-sized medals were worn. At first it was suggested that the ribbon be worn on the right breast along with the Presidential Unit Citation and the Navy Unit Citation; however, this was seen as presenting a problem because only unit awards were to be worn on the right breast and the addition of more ribbons was thought to produce a cluttered appearance. It was recommended that a medal be created to go with the SECNAV Commendation for Achievement, and that the medal be worn under appropriate circumstances. The Chief of Naval Operations accepted this proposal and recommended to the Secretary of the Navy that a medal be established to go with the ribbon. The proposal was favorably indorsed by the Navy Board of Decorations and Medals on June 16, 1964, and was approved by the Secretary of the Navy on June 22, 1964. On December 7, 1964, the name of the award was officially changed to the SECNAV Commendation for Achievement Medal. On July 17, 1967, it was again changed, this time to Navy Achievement Medal.

The Navy Achievement Medal is awarded to enlisted and commissioned members of the Navy and Marine Corps, including members of reserve components on active or inactive duty, who are in the grade of lieutenant commander/major or below for either outstanding achievement or meritorious service performed on or after May 1, 1961. It may also be awarded to members of other branches of the Armed Forces of comparable grade or rate, when attached to, or serving with, units of the Department of the Navy. The medal is awarded for outstanding achievement or for meritorious service (in combat or non-combat situations) based on sustained performance or specific achievement of a superlative nature which warrants more tangible recognition than is possible by a fitness report, but which does not warrant award of a Navy Commendation Medal. The professional achievement must clearly exceed that which is normally required or expected, considering the individual's grade or rate, training, and experience. Leadership which merits the award must be noteworthy and must be sustained so as to demonstrate a high state of development or, if for a specific achievement, be of such merit as to earn singular recognition, and must reflect most credibly on the efforts of the individual toward the accomplishment of the unit mission. The Navy Achievement Medal cannot be awarded for service involving aerial flight subsequent to January 1, 1969.

The design of the Navy Achievement Medal was suggested by the flag of the Secretary of the Navy. The actual design of the medal was done by Arnold P. Simmons and sculpted by Lewis J. King, Jr., of the Institute of Heraldry. The medal is rectangular in shape with clipped corners. In the center of the medal there is a fouled anchor, and in each corner there is a five-pointed star, single point up. The reverse of the medal is blank. The ribbon is myrtle green (suggested by the Navy Commendation Medal) with a stripe of Indian orange inside each edge of the ribbon.

Secretary of the Navy John B. Connally, whose interest in rewarding excellence in operations, administration, and management within the Navy resulted in the establishment of the Navy Achievement Medal. The other service branches and the Department of Defense followed suit and established their own Achievement Medals. (US Navy photo)

obverse

reverse

USAF Achievement Medal

THE AIR FORCE ACHIEVEMENT MEDAL

In June of 1978 Captain Robert C. Bonn, Jr., an officer assigned to the Recognition Programs Branch of the Air Force Manpower and Personnel Center (AFMPC), submitted a self-initiated study which proposed the creation of an Air Force Achievement Medal. He suggested the proposed Achievement Medal follow the Commendation Medal in precedence. Interestingly enough, in 1957 the Air Force had proposed to the other services that a medal to be known as the "Achievement Medal" be created and that it fall between the Legion of Merit and the service commendation medals. This proposal was not adopted, but a similar medal was created in 1969 with the establishment of the Meritorious Service Medal.

Captain Bonn's proposal was motivated by three factors. The first was that there were few award opportunities for the younger personnel who had entered the Air Force since the end of the Vietnam War. He felt that a decoration oriented toward this segment of the Air Force population would help remedy the problem. The second reason was the need to strengthen the position of the Commendation Medal. Because the Commendation Medal had to serve a wide spectrum of ranks and levels of performance, it suffered from a declining prestige as its use proliferated. In some cases, individuals scheduled to receive the Commendation Medal for retirement recognition would either decline it or return it to the Air Force. Captain Bonn felt that an Achievement Medal with liberal award criteria, directed at junior members of the Air Force, would restore the prestige of the Commendation Medal to the level it had previously enjoyed. Finally, Bonn proposed the establishment of an Achievement Medal so the Air Force would have a decoration comparable to the Achievement Medals of the Navy and Coast Guard (at this time neither the Army nor the Defense Department had established their respective Achievement Medals).

Captain Bonn proposed the Achievement Medal be awarded to enlisted personnel and to officers below the grade of lieutenant colonel. He further proposed that it not be used for retirement recognition to avoid retiree disatisfaction at receiving the lowest decoration available. He further proposed that it not be awarded for combat action or for acts of heroism. He envisioned the Achievement Medal as a noncombat award for meritorious service based on sustained performance, leadership, or for some specific achievement of a superlative nature.

Although it was not adopted in 1978, Captain Bonn's proposal was resurrected as part of a 1980 "top-to-bottom" analysis of the Air Force decoration program. This analysis was prompted by high-level interest in optimizing award opportunities in the post-Vietnam War era. The 1980 study found that the major concepts behind the Air Force awards program had not changed in its essentials since the 1949 joint service study that developed basic award policies and procedures. The 1980 study also traced the history of the problem of awards proliferation, noting that the lower the delegation of award authority, the greater the proliferation of the decoration. For this reason the Air Force had resisted all requests after the Vietnam War to delegate award authority below the major command level. While this greatly curtailed award proliferation, it still left many unit-level commanders frustrated at not possessing award authority for a decoration that could be quickly processed at the local level.

The 1980 study resurrected Captain Bonn's 1978 Achievement Medal proposal to remedy the finding that there was a need for increased recognition for lower ranking officers and junior enlisted personnel. The Achievement Medal also provided an answer to the need for a timely decoration that could be approved and awarded by a unit commander. In addtion, the study shared Captain Bonn's conviction that the Achievement Medal would restore prestige to the Commendation Medal and other, higher decorations. The study also felt the establishment of an Achievement Medal would have a favorable impact on morale and espirite-de-corps. While the study adopted Captain Bonn's concept, his recommended criteria were modified. The highest rank eligible for the Achievement Medal was increased to lieutenant colonel, and it was decided that the Achievement Medal be awarded for acts of heroism below that which would justify a Commendation Medal. His recommendation that it not be given for retirement recognition was retained, and an important provision was added: that it could not be awarded more than once a year to a given individual (to preclude adverse impact on the Air Force enlisted promotion system which assigns promotion points for decorations).

The study recommendations were approved, and on October 20, 1980, the Air Force Achievement Medal was established at the direction of Secretary of the Air Force Verne Orr. Unlike all other Air Force decorations, the Air Force Achievement Medal does not derive from an earlier Army decoration. As a result, it is the first decoration established under Air Force authority for Air Force personnel. The Air Force Achievement Medal is currently awarded for outstanding achievement or meritorious service rendered specifically on behalf of the Air Force. It may also be awarded for acts of heroism which do not meet the requirements for award of the Commendation Medal. It is restricted to the recognition of achievements and services that are clearly outstanding and unmistakably exceptional when compared to similar achievements and accomplishments of personnel of like rank and responsibilities. It may not be awarded for aerial achievement or retirement recognition (to prevent recognizing a full career with the decoration which occupies the lowest precedence), nor may it be awarded to an officer of the rank of colonel or higher.

A1C Heidi M. Uttrich receives the first Air Force Achievement Medal from Col. Carl D. Wall, at Brooks AFB, Texas. The medal used in the ceremony was a prototype model and was taken back after the picture was taken! (USAF photo)

A design proposal for the Air Force Achievement Medal was included by Captain Bonn in his 1978 study and was subsequently accepted. Since Captain Bonn had originally only proposed the obverse design, the reverse was completed by the Institute of Heraldry. Bonn proposed his own design because of his desire to present a complete proposal package and because he felt that as an amature artist his work was of a quality at least comparable to the designs of other decorations done by the Institute of Heraldry. Bonn's design was sculpted by Donald Borja of the Institute of Heraldry. The medal is a circular convex satin-oxidized, silver-colored disc using heraldic features of the shield of the Air Force Seal. In the center of the obverse is a heraldic thunderbolt in low relief which signifies striking power through the medium of aerospace. The disc is surrounded by a border nebully which represents clouds and the firmament. Captain Bonn chose eleven "clouds" as the sum of 4 and 7, the digits of the year the Air Force was established. On the reverse, in raised letters, is the circular inscription, *AIR FORCE MERITORIOUS ACHIEVEMENT*, with *AIR FORCE* at the top of the circle. The center of the reverse is blank and may be used to engrave the recipient's name. The Achievement Medal ribbon was created during a brainstorm session by Master Sergeant William B. Dowling and Mr. Ruben Cortinas, both assigned to the AFMPC Recognition Programs Branch. The ribbon consists of three sets of four vertical stripes of ultramarine blue over a silver-gray background. The colors have no meaning except to give the medal a distinctive "Air Force" appearance.

The first recipient of the Air Force Achievement Medal was A1C Heidi M. Uttrich of the 6570th Air Base Group, Brooks Air Force Base, Texas, who received her medal in early 1982.

Captain Robert C. Bonn, Jr., USAF. Captain Bonn's original proposal for an Air Force Achievement Medal was first turned down and then later accepted. His proposal included a suggested design for the medal which was adopted.

obverse

reverse

Army Achievement Medal

THE ARMY ACHIEVEMENT MEDAL

For a number of years after the Vietnam War the Army was concerned about its overall distribution of awards and decorations. Numerous proposals had been received by the Military Personnel Center for adding to or modifying the awards system, but none seemed fully satisfactory. Although there was a widespread perception that *something* was needed, primarily for junior soldiers, it was not clear what that "something" was. The Army believed that the kind of recognition that was needed would have to be employed on a fairly large scale. However, the prospect of increasing the number of awards of currently authorized decorations did not appeal to senior personnel specialists, who felt that simply giving out more existing decorations would simply reduce the value of those decorations.

The various staffing efforts to come up with an acceptable solution did not produce a common base upon which a new award could be established, nor was there even a clear consensus on whether or not a new decoration was needed. The commanders who believed a new decoration was needed recommended awards and suggested qualifying criteria as varied as the commands they represented; moreover, their proposals tended to be restricted in scope and dealt with only the narrow needs of the persons making the recommendation. Each effort to create a new decoration became bogged down in trying to find meaningful criteria for the award, and as a result each proposal was disapproved because the needs of all commands could not be met.

On August 28, 1980, Major General Robert M. Elton of the Military Personnel Center sent a "decision memorandum" to the Army Chief of Staff in which he proposed a solution to the problem. General Elton said that he believed the previous efforts were unsuccessful because they all attempted to solve the problem without adequately defining just what it was. He felt that the underlying problem was that, "...the current awards do not provide the means to meet the perceived needs for recognition to junior soldiers." He came to the conclusion that several awards were needed to meet the needs of all commands and that a single award would not suffice. He went on to recommend that the Army establish an Achievement Medal similar to that of the Navy and Air Force, and that three additional new ribbons be created: an Overseas Service Ribbon, an Army Basic Professional Training Ribbon, and an NCO Professional Development Ribbon. Finally, he recommended that Army personnel be authorized to wear any foreign badges they had been awarded (Army regulations prohibited the wearing of any such badges if they were awarded after September 1, 1975).

The criteria for the proposed Army Achievement Medal provided that it would be awarded to Army personnel for significant achievement not considered adequate to qualify for the Army Commendation Medal but which none the less deserved recognition. Award authority was to be vested in commanders in the grade of O-6 (Colonel) in order to make it a less cumbersome and time-consuming decoration to get approved and awarded. Finally, it was recommended that the Achievement Medal be limited to noncombat achievement and that members of other branches of the Armed Forces be eligible for it under certain circumstances. On April 10, 1981, the recommendation was approved by the Army Chief of Staff and the decoration was accordingly established by Secretary of the Army John O. Marsh on April 10, 1981.

The Army Achievement Medal is awarded to any member of the Armed Forces who, while serving in any capacity with the Army in a noncombat area on or after August 1, 1981, distinguishes himself by outstanding achievement or by meritorious service of a lesser degree than that required for award of the Army Commendation Medal. The Army Achievement Medal may not be awarded to an officer in the grade of general.

The medal was designed by Jay Morris and sculpted by Donald Borja, both of the Army's Institute of Heraldry. Although the design of the Army Achievement Medal was approved by the Commission on Fine Arts on May 29, 1981, their approval was given with some hesitation. In a letter to the Institute of Heraldry, the Secretary of the Commission on Fine Arts noted that "After considerable discussion, the Commission members voted to approve the submission, although they did so with some reluctance. They do not feel that the design is particularly distinguished and hope that future medals will be of a higher caliber."

The medal is a bronze octagon one and one half inches in diameter with one angle at top, centered. On the obverse is a design consisting of elements of the Department of the Army Seal. On the reverse, in three lines, are the words, *FOR MILITARY ACHIEVEMENT* above a space for inscription of the recipient's name and below which are two slips of laurel. The ribbon consists of green, white, and ultramarine stripes.

The design on the obverse is a symbol which emphasizes the Army's heritage. On the reverse the words denote the purpose of the award. The laurel is the traditional symbol of achievement.

Major General Robert M. Elton, U.S. Army. General Elton proposed the establishment of the Army Achievement Medal to provide recognition to lower ranking soldiers. (US Army photo)

obverse

reverse

USCG Achievement Medal

THE COAST GUARD ACHIEVEMENT MEDAL

Following the lead of the Secretary of the Navy (who established the "Secretary of the Navy Commendation for Achievement with Ribbon" in 1961, which was subsequently designated the Navy Achievement Medal), the Secretary of the Treasury established a similar ribbon for Coast Guard personnel on January 29, 1964. The Commandant of the Coast Guard formally redesignated the ribbon as the Coast Guard Achievement Medal on June 11, 1968.

The Coast Guard Achievement Medal may be awarded to all members of the Coast Guard, including reserves, as well as to members of other branches of the Armed Forces when serving with Coast Guard units. It is given for professional or leadership achievement in either peacetime or combat situations. It may be awarded based on sustained performance or for specific achievement of a superlative nature, but not of a level which would more appropriately justify award of a Commendation Medal or other decoration.

The Coast Guard Achievement Medal was designed by Irving Lyons and sculpted by Lewis J. King, Jr., both of the Army's Institute of Heraldry. It is a bronze disc in the center of which is the Coast Guard Seal surrounded by a laurel wreath, which is in turn surrounded by a border of cable. The reverse bears the inscription (in raised letters), *AWARDED TO* in the upper portion and *FOR ACHIEVEMENT* in the lower. The ribbon is the same as that of the Navy Achievement Medal except that it has a narrow pinstripe of white in the center of the ribbon.

Symbolically, the laurel wreath represents achievement and the continuous cable stands for fidelity of the seaman in support of the Coast Guard, which is represented by the Coast Guard Seal.

obverse

reverse

Purple Heart Medal

THE PURPLE HEART

The Purple Heart is the oldest American military decoration, originally established as the Badge of Military Merit by General George Washington on August 7, 1782. In his Order of the Day establishing the Badge of Military Merit, Washington issued the following directive:

> The General, ever desirous to cherish a virtuous ambition in his soldiers, as well as to foster and encourage every species of Military Merit, directs that whenever any singularly meritorious action is performed, the author of it shall be permitted to wear on his facings, over his left breast, the figure of a heart in purple cloth, or silk, edged with narrow lace or binding. Not only instances of unusual gallantry but also of extraordinary fidelity and essential service in any way shall meet with a due reward....
>
> The road to glory in a patriot army and a free country is thus opened to all. This order is also to have retrospect to the earliest days of the war, and to be considered as a permanent one.

Washington's Badge of Military Merit was referred to as the *Purple Heart*, and it is interesting to speculate on how he came upon the idea of using a purple heart to reward his most deserving soldiers. It is known that in Washington's time "*purpleheart*" alluded to the carriage in which certain guns were mounted. "Purpleheart" is also a very handsome smooth-grained wood of a rich plum color which was especially adaptable for use with firearms and artillery. The wood was held in high esteem by military engineers of Washington's time because it was believed to be the best wood in the world for mortar beds and gun carriages because it could withstand violent stress better than any other type of wood. Purpleheart, which is a species of *Peltogyne*, is stronger than oak and is highly resistant to wood-destroying fungi and wood termites. Its principle source is tropical America, from Mexico to Brazil, although it is most abundant in the Amazon basin and the Guianas - a region between the Amazon and the Orinoco Rivers in northeast South America. Perhaps Washington wished for all to recognize the recipients of the Badge of Military Merit as the sturdiest and most reliable of soldiers.

There are only three known awards of the original Badge of Military Merit, although it is possible that others were awarded. It should be noted that it was not then considered a badge to be given for wounds suffered in combat, but rather a high decoration for valor. In reality, the Purple Heart was the forerunner of the Medal of Honor.

ELIJAH CHURCHILL

The first Badge of Military Merit went to Sergeant Elijah Churchill of the Fourth Troop, 2nd Regiment of Light Dragoons. Based on intelligence gathered from well-placed spies, it was learned in November of 1780 that the British had stored a large quantity of hay for winter forage near Coram (Long Island), New York. The forage was protected by a small fortification consisting of three blockhouses connected by a stockade of heavy twelve-foot long stakes sharpened on the end. The fortification was also protected by a ditch, a high wall, and a series of bent trees which were sharpened on the end and pointed in the direction of any would-be attackers. This fortification was named Fort St. George.

Washington approved plans for an assault on Fort St. George and assigned the task to Major Benjamin Tallmadge of the Second Regiment of Light Dragoons. Tallmadge formed a raiding party of fifty men, including Sergeant Churchill. The group marched to Fairfield, Connecticut, which was opposite the point on Long Island where they wished to land. Because of a violent gale, the raiding party was forced to wait eight days before making its crossing. At four o'clock in the afternoon of November 21, 1780, they crossed the Long Island Sound in whale boats. Once on Long Island they were in danger of being discovered by a large force of British Regulars quartered on the island - or by numerous loyalist troops scattered about the area.

By November 23, 1780, the raiding party was within two miles of Fort St. George. The party was divided into three groups and each was assigned to attack a specific blockhouse. Sergeant Churchill was placed in charge of sixteen men and ordered to attack the main (and largest) blockhouse. The assault began at four o'clock in the morning, and the raiders got to within fifty feet of the fort before they were discovered by British sentinels. Churchill's party stormed the central blockhouse before its defenders could organize their resistance. However, a British schooner at anchor near the fort began to fire on the raiders, so a group was detached to capture the ship, which they did in short order. The fort, the schooner, and the winter forage - over three hundred tons of hay - were set on fire, and by four o'clock in the afternoon the raiders and their prisoners reached their boats. By eleven o'clock in the evening of November 23, 1780, the raiders and their fifty English prisoners were back in Fairfield, Connecticut.

The second incident upon which Churchill's Purple Heart was based also involved a raid on Long Island. Washington had become annoyed by a fort the British had built on the north shore of Long Island, about forty-eight miles northeast of Brooklyn, which they called Fort Slongo. Major Tallmadge was again charged with leading an attack on the fort. For this operation, he formed a force of about one hundred men, including the intrepid Sergeant Churchill; however, this particular raid was to be led by Major Lemuel Trescott of the Ninth Massachusetts Regiment, who had volunteered for the task. The raiding party started across Long Island Sound at eight o'clock in the evening of October 2, 1781, and quickly launched a direct attack on the fort. By three in the morning the fort was captured with no losses and with the capture of twenty-one prisoners. For his participation in these two raids, Sgt. Churchill was awarded the Badge of Military Merit. At the time of his second exploit he was twenty-six years old. He served in the Continental Army until the end of the war and then moved to Chester, Massachusetts, where he died on April 11, 1841, at the age of eighty-eight.

WILLIAM BROWN

The second person to receive the Purple Heart was Sergeant William Brown of the Fifth Regiment, Connecticut Line. Brown, who was born at Stamford, Connecticut on February 12, 1761, earned his Purple Heart at Yorktown on October 14, 1781. A siege by the Americans and French had become stalled by two strong British "redoubts" (fortifications). The Americans attacked the outer redoubt, led by Sergeant Brown, in what was then referred to as a "forlorn hope" because by leading the attacking party, he had virtually no hope of coming out alive. The assault was made under the command of Lt. Col. Alexander Hamilton and Brown led by charging over formidable obstacles and into the fortification in the face of a murderous fire. In less than fifteen minutes the redoubt was captured and Brown miraculously escaped death or injury. Washington was so impressed with his courage that he subsequently awarded Brown the Purple Heart on April 24, 1783. After the war Brown moved to Cincinnati, Ohio, where he died in 1808 at the age of forty-seven.

DANIEL BISSELL

The third Purple Heart was awarded to Sergeant Daniel Bissell, who was born at Windsor, Connecticut on December 30, 1754. It was awarded for a saga which started in August of 1781 when Washington decided that he needed detailed and accurate information on British units in New York City. Sergeant Bissell was selected for the job and succeeded in getting behind British lines and in gathering the information Washington needed. Unfortunately, he could not get back out to report his information. He remained behind the lines for a year, acting as a British soldier, having joined the British army in order to avoid being conscripted into their navy. He worked as a quartermaster sergeant and served in various camps and hospitals, thereby avoiding having to engage in direct combat with his own countrymen. All the time Bissell was in the British Army he continued to gather intelligence information and made voluminous notes on what he gathered.

The British, however, became suspicious of spies and ordered that anyone caught with written information on his person be considered a spy and hanged. Fearful of discovery, Bissell destroyed his notes. He was finally able to make good his escape in September of 1782 and went straight to Washington's headquarters. He gave a detailed report on the forts on Staten Island and provided descriptions and sketches of the forts in New York City and on Long Island. His handwritten report was personally endorsed by Washington. Washington's General Order for June 8, 1783, cite Bissell for the Purple Heart and state that, "Sergeant Bissell of the 2nd Connecticut Regiment, having performed some important services within the immediate knowledge of the Commander-in-Chief, in which the fidelity, perseverance and good sense of the said Sergt. Bissell were conspicuously manifested; it is therefore ordered that he be honored with the badge of Merit; he will call at Head Quarters on Tuesday next for the insignia and certificate to which he is hereby entitled."

After the war he settled in Randolph, Vermont, and later moved to Richmond, New York, where he died on August 5, 1824, at sixty-nine years of age. Sergeant Bissell's Purple Heart and certificate were destroyed in July of 1813 when his house burned and all of his personal effects were lost. As an interesting footnote, in 1952 2nd Lt John J. Bissell of Pittsburgh, Pennsylvania, a direct descendant of Daniel Bissell, won the Purple Heart for wounds he received at "Bunker Hill" in Korea.

After the Revolution the Badge of Military Merit fell into disuse and was all but forgotten for almost a hundred and fifty years. In 1931, General Douglas MacArthur, who was then War Department Chief of Staff, approved a proposal that the Badge of Military Merit be restored as an Army decoration and that it be officially designated as the Purple Heart Medal. Accordingly, on the two-hundredth anniversary of George Washington's birth (February 22, 1932), the Purple Heart Medal was established by War Department

General Order Number 3. The early issues of the Purple Heart Medal were serially numbered on the rim, and Purple Heart #1 was awarded to General MacArthur on July 21, 1932 (the first Purple Heart Medal which was actually presented - medal number #4 - was awarded to Major General Harry L. Gilchrist on April 28, 1932).

At the time the Purple Heart Medal was established the Navy took the position that it was a purely Army decoration and did not authorize it for award to Navy or Marine Corps personnel. However, on December 3, 1942, President Franklin D. Roosevelt extended the Purple Heart to members of the Navy, Marine Corps, and Coast Guard and made it retroactive to December 6, 1941. The first Coast Guardsman to receive the Purple Heart was Chief Boatswain's Mate Lloyd M. Morris who received his medal for wounds he sustained during landing operations in North Africa. It is not known who the first Navy recipient was. In 1952 President Harry Truman made the Purple Heart retroactive to April 5, 1917, for all services, thus allowing servicemen wounded in World War I to receive the medal. In 1962 President John F. Kennedy extended eligibility for the Purple Heart to any civilian national of the United States who, while serving under competent authority in any capacity with a branch of the armed forces, was wounded.

Prior to February 22, 1932, award of the Purple Heart was confined to those persons, who as members of the Army, were awarded the Meritorious Services Citation Certificate by the Commander-in-Chief, American Expeditionary Forces, or who were wounded in action in any war or campaign under conditions which would entitle them to wear a wound chevron. Since February 22, 1932 (as amended by various laws and Executive Orders), the Purple Heart may only be awarded for wounds, injuries, or death suffered after April 5, 1917, by any person serving with the armed forces under any one of the following conditions: (1) in any action against an enemy of the United States, (2) in any action with an opposing armed force of a foreign country in which the armed forces of the United States are or have been engaged, (3) while serving with friendly foreign forces engaged in an armed conflict against an opposing armed force in which the United States is not a belligerent party, (4) as the direct result of an act by any hostile foreign force, (5) while serving outside the territory of the United States after March 28, 1973, as part of a peacekeeping force, or (6) if wounded or killed after March 28, 1973, as a result of international terrorist attack against the United States or a foreign nation friendly to the United States.

The injury or wound must require treatment by a medical officer and the treatment must be a matter of record. A person who is wounded, injured, or killed as a result of a parachute jump or an aircraft disabled by hostile fire, or who is wounded, injured, or killed by captors while in a prisoner of war status qualifies for award of the Purple Heart.

It should be noted in passing that during the First World War there had been an effort to establish an award for wounds received in action. As a matter of fact, the Adjutant General recommended that a ribbon be authorized for each wound received in action. It was originally proposed that the design of the ribbon be the same as that of the Medal of Honor, substituting red (alluding to blood) for the blue (this ribbon was later adopted as the ribbon to the Marine Corps Brevet Medal). The final design, however, was a red ribbon with a narrow stripe of white in the center. The acting chief of the War College Division of the General Staff proposed this idea to the Secretary of War on August 6, 1917, and on September 6, 1917, Secretary of War Newton D. Baker directed a General Order be issued providing every officer and enlisted man who was "hereinafter wounded in action" be authorized to wear the ribbon for each wound, provided that not more than one ribbon be worn unless the wounds were received on different dates. Baker accepted the proposal for the red ribbon with the white stripe in the center and directed that it be worn on the right breast. War Department General Order Number 134 of October 12, 1917, authorized the ribbon; however, the order was rescinded 32 days later and the ribbon never became a reality. Instead the Army authorized "wound chevrons" which were to be worn on the sleeve of the tunic.

The original Badge of Military Merit was designed by Pierre Charles L'Enfant in accordance with Washington's personal instructions. The Purple Heart Medal was designed by Elizabeth Will of the Army's Institute of Heraldry. Miss Will's design was sculpted by John R. Sinnock. The medal takes the shape of a heart. The inner portion is purple (originally enamel, now plastic) edged in gold wash. In the center is a profile of George Washington in his uniform as Commander-in-Chief. Above the profile of Washington is his family crest containing two red horizontal bars beneath three stars on a field of white. On each side of the crest is a branch of laurel. The reverse is plain except for the words, *FOR MILITARY MERIT*.

The medal is an adaptation of L'Enfant's original design; however, in its revised format it not only alludes to strength and courage as Washington intended, but also to Washington himself through his profile on the obverse of the medal. Interestingly, the original Purple Heart designed by L'Enfant had two sprays of silver laurel inside the heart. When Miss Will first designed the Purple Heart Medal she featured two sprays of silver laurel on the obverse, but the Commission on Fine Arts rejected the design because it failed to suggest Washington. She then removed the laurel sprays and put Washington's profile in their place. The words on the reverse are derived from the original Badge of Military Merit. The ribbon is purple watered silk, edged in white.

BIBLIOGRAPHY

BOOKS

Abraham, Irwin R. *U.S. Merchant Marine Decorations and Awards.* Dolton, Illinois: by the author, 1966.

Belden, Bauman L. *United States War Medals.* New York: American Numismatic Society, 1916; reprint edition, Greenwhich, Connecticut: Norm Flayderman, 1962.

Blakeney, Jane. *Heroes, U.S. Marine Corps, 1861-1955.* Washington, D.C.: by the author, 1957.

Floyd, Jeffrey B. *For Extraordinary Heroism: The Air Force Cross.* Alexandria, Virginia: by the author, 1982.

Fry, James B. *The History and Legal Effects of Brevets.* New York: D. Van Nostrand, Publisher, 1877.

Gleim, Albert F. *The Certificate of Merit, U.S. Army Distinguished Service Award: 1847-1918.* Alexandria, Virginia: by the author, 1979.

Johnson, Stanley C. *The Medal Collector.* New York: Dodd Mead and Company, 1921 (see chapter XVI).

Kerrigan, Evans E. *American War Medals and Decorations,* revised edition. New York: The Viking Press, 1971.

Kerrigan, Evans E. *The Sea Shall Not Have Them.* Norton Heights, Connecticut: Medallic Publishing Company, 1971.

Kittredge, Tracy Barrett. *Naval Lessons of the Great War.* Garden City: Doubleday, Page and Company, 1921; see especially Chapter IV, "The Daniels Medal Awards," pp. 41-73.

Morgan, Joseph M. *Military Medals and Insignia of the United States.* Glendale, California: Griffin-Patterson Publishing Company, 1941.

Peterson, Gordon. *A Guide to U.S. Army Insignia and Decorations.* New York, 1972.

Pullen, John J. *A Shower of Stars.* Philadelphia: J.B. Lippincott Company, 1966.

Purves, Alec A. *The Medals, Decorations and Orders of the Great War: 1914-1918.* London: J.B. Hayward and Son, 1975.

Riley, David. *Uncommon Valor...* Marceline, Missouri: by the author, 1980.

Rodenbough, Theodore F. *Uncle Sam's Medal of Honor.* New York: G.P. Putnam's Sons, 1886.

Robles, Philip K. *United States Military Medals and Ribbons.* Rutland, Vermont: Charles E. Tuttle Company, 1971.

Rosignoli, Guido. *Ribbons of Orders, Decorations and Medals.* New York: Arco Publishing Company, 1977.

Stringer, Harry R., ed. *Distinguished Service.* Washington, DC: Fassett Publishing Company, 1921.

Stringer, Harry R. *Heroes All.* Washington, DC: Fassett Publishing Company, 1919.

Werlich, Robert. *Orders and Decorations of all Nations, Ancient and Modern, Civil and Military,* 2d ed. Washington, DC: Quaker Press, 1974.

Willoughby, Malcolm F. *The U.S. Coast Guard in World War II.* Annapolis, Maryland: United States Naval Institute Press, 1957 (see especially Appendix A, "Medals and Awards").

Wyllie, Robert E. *Orders, Decorations and Insignia, Military and Civil.* New York: G.P. Putnams's Sons, 1921.

GOVERNMENT DOCUMENTS

D'Acosta, Uriel P. "The Necessity For a Separate United States Air Force Decorations System," Unpublished Staff Study, Air Command and Staff College, Maxwell AFB, Alabama, March 1948.

Penrod, David J. "United States Military Decorations," Unpublished Staff Study, Armed Forces Staff College, October 30, 1972.

United States, The Commission on Fine Arts, *Eighth Report January 1, 1918 - July 1, 1919.* Washington, D.C.: Government Printing Office, 1920. See especially "The Great War," pp. 25-39.

U.S. Congress, Senate. Committee on Veteran's Affairs. *Medal of Honor Recipients: 1863-1973.* Committee Print Number 15, 93rd Congress, 1st Session, 1973.

U.S. Congress, Senate. Subcommittee on Naval Affairs. *Awarding Medals in the Naval Service,* Hearings Before A Senate Subcommittee on Naval Affairs on S. Res. 285, 66th Congress, 2nd Session, 1920.

U.S. War Department, Office of the Adjutant General. *Decorations, United States Army: 1862-1926.* Washington, D.C.: Government Printing Office, 1927. See also Supplements I through V.

ARTICLES

Abraham, Irwin R. "The Distinguished Service Cross." *The Medal Collector* 20 (July 1969): 3-9 (ill).

Abraham, Irwin R. "Vietnam Service Bar for American Merchant Marine." *The Medal Collector* 31 (October 1980): 32.

"Air Medals." *Popular Science* 151 (May 24, 1947): 104 (ill).

Allen, C.B. "Bravery vs Ballyhoo." *Outlook* 157 (January 7, 1931): 12-14 (ill).

"American Decorations and Insignia of Honor and Service." *National Geographic* 36 (December 1919): 502-526 (ill).

"American Soldiers and Foreign Decorations." *Outlook* 118 (January 16, 1918): 81-82.

"Army and Navy Medals." *Newsweek* 20 (September 21, 1942): 65.

"Army and Navy Medals." *New York Times Magazine* (June 21, 1942): 20:21 (ill).

Ayres, Anthony R. "The West Indies Naval Campaign Medal 1898 and its Engagements." *The Medal Collector* 21 (July 1970): 10-16 (ill).

"Badges of Courage for our Men." *Literary Digest* 55 (December 15, 1917): 11.

"Beautiful Medals are Offered by Uncle Sam." *Popular Mechanics* 56 (July 1931): 63.

Bishop, Lee. "Honors and Awards of the United States Merchant Marine." *The Medal Collector* 33 (July 1982): 4-24 (ill).

Bradford, Braxton. "The Specially Meritorious Service Medal, Spanish American War." *The Medal Collector* 32 (November 1981): 11-12 (ill).

Brook, Vernon R. "Bronze Star for World War II Combat Badges." *The Medal Collector* 30 (May 1979): 4-9 (ill).

Brown, Frank C. and Vernon Brook. "Sino-American Co-operative Organization Commemorative Medal." *The Medal Collector* 26 (September 1975): 32-33 (ill).

Cannon, Brian G. "Development of the United States Marine Corps Expeditonary Medal," *The Medal Collector* 32 (October 1981): 14-15 (ill).

Cartafalsa, John B. "U.S. Army Decorations and Awards." *The Medal Collector* 32 (November 1981): 7.

"Carter Orders Military Decoration." *The Medal Collector* 29 (January 1978): 21. Deals with the Defense Meritorious Service Medal.

Chamberlain, G.S. "American Medals." *Hobbies* 55 (September 1950): 137-138 (ill).

"Decorations and Service Ribbons of U.S. Armed Forces." *Life* 15 (October 4, 1943): 76-78 (ill).

"Decorations, Medals and Ribbons." *All Hands* (November 1944): 34-41.

"Distinguished Flying Cross Awarded to Wright Brothers." *New York Times* (February 28, 1929): 2:6.

"Distinguished Service Cross Medal." *The Army and Navy Register* LXX (September 3, 1921): 227.

DuBois, Arthur E. "The Heraldry of Heroism." *The National Geographic Magazine* LXXXIV (October 1943): 409-444. (ill).

DuBoise, Arthur E. "U.S. Military Heraldry." *Quartermaster Review* 28 (March 1949): 42-43; 109-110.

Evans, Hoyt C. "How Many Occupation Medals?" *The Medal Collector* 31 (January/February 1980): 18-19 (ill).

Evans, Hoyt C. "The Medals of 1942," *The Medal Collector* 33 (March 1982): 4-8.

Evans, Hoyt C. "The Russian Railway Service Corps and the Victory Medal." *The Medal Collector* 28 (December 1977): 24-25 (ill).

Farek, Daniel J. "An Analysis of the Indian Wars Campaign Medal Roll." *The Medal Collector* 26 (January 1975): 28-29.

Farek, Daniel J. "Sampson Medal Roll - USS Abarenda." *The Medal Collector* 31 (June 1980): 24.

Farek, Daniel J. "Sampson Medal Roll - USS Alvarado." *The Medal Collector* 31 (November 1980): 28.

Farek, Daniel J. "Sampson Medal Roll - USS Fern." *The Medal Collector* 31 (January/February 1980): 23.

Farek, Daniel J. "Sampson Medal Roll - USS Alexander Hamilton." *The Medal Collector* 32 (June 1981): 17.

Farek, Daniel J. "Sampson Medal Roll - USS Ericsson." *The Medal Collector* 29 (August 1978): 21.

Farek, Daniel J. "Sampson Medal Roll - USS Hawk." *The Medal Collector* 34 (December 1983): 16.

Farek, Daniel J. "Sampson Medal Roll - USS McKee." *The Medal Collector* 32 (December 1981): 23.

Farek, Daniel J. "Sampson Medal Roll - USS Morrill." *The Medal Collector* 34 (January/February 1983): 11-12.

Farek, Daniel J. "Sampson Medal Roll - USS Porter." *The Medal Collector* 30 (February 1979): 24.

Farek, Daniel J. "Sampson Medal Roll - USS Winslow." *The Medal Collector* 29 (January 1978): 24.

Fegan, J.C. "The Purple Heart Badge and the Order of Military Merit." *The Marine Corps Gazette* 2 (August 1932): 39-44.

"First Award of Korea Service Ribbon; United Nations Service Medal." *U.N. Bulliten* 11 (December 1, 1951): 441 (ill).

Fischer, Ronald E. "Some New U.S. Armed Forces Awards." *The Medal Collector* 28 (February 1977): 11-15 (ill). Discusses the Defense Distinguished Service Medal and the Defense Superior Service Medal.

Floyd, Jeffrey B. "New Decorations and Ribbons Authorized." *The Medal Collector* 32 (April 1981): 24 (il,); notes Air Force Achievement Medal (see also addendum: vol 32, number 10, October 1981, p. 28).

Friederich, Rudolf J. "Distinguished Service Medal - USAF." *The Medal Collector* 20 (March 1969): 3.

Genders, Anne "The Purple Heart." *Soldiers* 37 (August 1982): 38-40 (ill).

Gleim, Albert F. "The Army of Puerto Rican Occupation Badge." *The Medal Collector* 31 (March 1980): 4-9 (ill).

Gleim, Albert F. "The China Service Medal." *The Medal Collector* 30 (August 1979): 4-10 (ill).

Gleim, Albert F. "Congressional Texas Cavalry Medal." *The Medal Collector* 23 (November 1972): 3-7 (ill).

Gleim, Albert F. "Fakes and Copies, No. 3." *The Medal Collector* 29 (December 1978): 19.

Gleim, Albert F. "The 1915 Haitian Campaign Medal." *The Medal Collector* 30 (June 1979): 8-10 (ill).

Gleim, Albert F. "Issue of Marine Corps Service Medals to Army Personnel." *The Medal Collector* 22 (December 1971): 12.

Gleim, Albert F. "Numbering of U.S. Army Campaign Medals." *The Medal Collector* 22 (June 1971): 2-8.

Gleim, Albert F. "The U.S. Army Medal Designs of Francis D. Millet." *The Medal Collector* 22 (April 1971): 14-18 (ill).

Gleim, Albert F. and William H. Powers. "U.S. Army Campaign Medal Rim Numbering 1907-1942." *The Medal Collector* 31 (May 1980): 19-22 (ill).

Gray, John A. "An Expeditionary Medal." *The Marine Corps Gazette* 3 (September 1928): 164-165.

Halpin, Thomas S., Jr. "The Numbering of United States Campaign Medals." *The Medal Collector* 22 (June 1971): 9-11.

Haynes, Edward S. "The Development of United States Army Campaign Badges, 1900-1907: An Introduction." *The Medal Collector* 22 (July 1971): 10:12.

Haynes, Edward S. "F.D. Millet's Original Designs for U.S. Army Campaign Badges." *The Medal Collector* 22 (December 1971): 16-17.

Haynes, Edward S. "Numbered U.S. Army Campaign Medals Awarded to Members of the U.S. Marine Corps - A Preliminary Report." *The Medal Collector* 22 (July 1971): 8-10.

Haynes, Edward S. "A Preliminary Medal Roll of the United States Marine Corps Badge for the Civil War, 1861-1865." *The Medal Collector* 22 (June 1971): 26-28.

Haynes, Edward S. "U.S. Marine Corps Recipients of the Dewey Medal." *The Medal Collector* 27 (September 1976): 23-27.

Haynes, Edward S. "The United States Marine Corps Brevet Medal and its Recipients." *The Medal Collector* 23 (May 1972): 3-20 (ill).

"Heroes of the Flying Cross." *Popular Mechanics* 64 (October 1935): 568-570 (ill).

Hess, Edward V. "Korea Service Medal." *The Medal Collector* 20 (September 1969): 10-12.

Hopkins, A.A. "Military Decorations of Our Fighting Men." *Scientific American* 117 (December 15, 1917): 456 (ill).

Hopkins, A.A. "Pomp and Circumstances." *Scientific American* 4 (September 1921): 228-234 (ill).

"How Medals are Made." *Popular Science* 143 (July 1943): 61 (ill).

Hoytash, C. "History of Decorations and Medals." *Hobbies* 51 (July 1946): 104.

Hume, Edgar H. "The Medical Book of Merit: United States Army and Navy Decorations Awarded to Medical Officers for Distinguished Service in the World War." *The Military Surgeon* 56 (March 1925): 241-308.

Kenworthy, Jane. "United States Navy Medals of Honor Unclaimed or Withheld." *Medal of Honor History Roundtable*, 1976 (mimeo).

Kosier, Edwin J. "The Air Force Cross." *The Medal Collector* 19 (May 1968): 28-30.

Krug, Gary C. "Notes on U.S. Federal Awards: Number 1 - Dominican Campaign Medal, 1916, Navy Issue." *The Medal Collector* 23 (September 1972): 28-30.

Krug, Gary C. "Varieties of the U.S. Air Medal." *The Medal Collector* 19 (April 1968): 2-3.

Krug, Gary C. "Varieties of the U.S. Army Distinguished Service Medal." *The Medal Collector* 16 (December 1965): 5-14 (ill).

Lelle, John E. "China War Memorial Badge and Ribbon - The Lost Decoration of World War II." *The Medal Collector* 26 (December 1975): 3-7 (ill).

Lelle, John E. "The United States Victory Medal of World War One." *The Medal Collector* 28 (April 1977): 4-34 (ill).

Lelle, John E. "1919 Victory Medal Clasps and U.S. Army Divisions." *The Medal Collector* 22 (July 1971): 13-15.

Long, Richard A. "Brevet Medal's Design was Informal Process." *Fortitudine* XII (Fall 1982): 21-22 (ill).

Long, Richard A. "The Marine Corps Brevet Medal." *The Medal Collector* 32 (November 1981): 28-29.

Lord, Cush. "United States of America Meritorious Service Medal." *The Medal Collector* 24 (March 1971): 4.

Magruder, J.H. III "The Brevet in the Marine Corps." *Marine Corps Gazette* 39 (November 1955): 54-57.

Marcosson, I.F. "Our Tribe of Ribbon Hunters." *American Mercury* 47 (July 1939): 268-274.

McConnell, Glenn A. "The Early Distinguished Flying Cross." *The Medal Collector* 34 (April 1983): 26-28.

McDowell, Charles P. "The Distinguished Service Cross in World War II." *The Medal Collector* 24 (March 1973): 25-29.

McDowell, Charles P. "Recipients of Multiple Awards of the Distinguished Service Cross Prior to World War II." *The Medal Collector* 24 (June 1973): 12-15.

McDowell, Charles P. "USAF Multiple Recipients of the Distinguished Service Cross." *The Medal Collector* 32 (October 1981): 17-19.

McNamara, David. "A Different Medal of Honor, Variety or Forgery?" *The Medal Collector* 25 (November 1974): 6-13 (ill).

"Medal for Berlin." *Newsweek* 44 (July 26, 1954): 42.

"Medal Factory." *Newsweek* 27 (March 11, 1946): 38.

"Medal is an Art, an Honor, A Collector's Item, A Small But Handsome Business." *Fortune* 31 (June 1945): 144-149 (ill).

"Medals and Insignia Authorized for U.S. Soldiers in France with Army Rules and Regulations Governing Their Bestowal." *U.S. Naval Institute Proceedings* 44 (May 1918): 1324-1326.

"Medals of Honor as a Recognition of Gallantry." *Harper's Weekly* 46 (April 12, 1902): 480.

"Nation's Gratitude." *New York Times Magazine* (November 25, 1951): 63.

"Naval Decorations." *Bureau of Navigation Bulletin No. 301* (April 1, 1942): 24-31.

"New Army Decorations and Medals." *Scientific American* 117 (December 15, 1917): 481 (ill).

"New Army Decoration: Silver Star Medal." *United States Army Recruiting News* 14 (September 13, 1932): 9.

Nihart, Franklin B. "The George Medal." *The Medal Collector* 25 (February 1974): 27-28 (ill).

"Not Only Gallantry: Newest U.S. Medal, The Legion of Merit." *Time* 40 (November 23, 1942): 82.

"On Medals." *Outlook* 124 (January 7, 1920): 14.

Perini, Michael B. "World War II Ace Receives Air Force Cross." *Air Force Magazine* 66 (August 1983): 29.

Peterson, Mendel L. "The Marine Corps Brevet Medal." *Numismatist* 64 (June 1951): 594-598.

Peterson, Mendel L. "The Navy Cross." *Numismatist* 65 (December 1952): 1170-1174.

Powell, D.E. "Double Winners of the Congressional Medal of Honor." *The Medal Collector* 22 (January 1971): 9-10.

"Presentation of the Badge of Merit to Sergeant Elijah Churchill by General George Washington." *American Artist* 29 (February 1965): 4 (ill).

"Purple Heart." *Science Newsletter* 44 (August 21, 1943): 117 (ill).

"Purple Heart Won by Descendant of Original Winner." *All Hands* (December 1952): 57.

Racine, Frank M. "Epic of Naval Aviation (The NC-4 Medal)." *The Medal Collector* 26 (January 1975): 3-22 (ill).

Rairden, Percy W., Jr. "Campaign and Service Medals - Their History and Tradition." *United States Naval Institute Proceedings* 75 (May 1949): 515.

Ranck, E.C. "American Military Decorations." *Current History Magazine, New York Times* part 2 (September 1919): 472-476.

Richards, George "Naval and Military Decorations." *United States Naval Institute Proceedings* 57 (May 1931): 575-583 (ill).

Ross, F.C. "Medals As Custodians of History." *Hobbies* 51 (October 1946): 98.

Shelton, Michael W. "Who are the Heroes?" *Naval Institute Proceedings* 104 (August 1978): 41-49.

Shelton, W.H. "War Medals." *Scribner's Magazine* 63 (February 1918): 252-256 (ill).

"Signs of Action: American Fighters Earn More Than 3,838 Medals." *Time* 40 (December 21, 1942): 86 (ill).

Silvernail, Robert G. "How The Air Force Cross Began." *The Medal Collector* 21 (August 1970): 29-30.

Strong, Robert W. "The Texas Cavalry Service Medal." *The Medal Collector* 23 (November 1972): 7-8.

Till, Paul H. "The American Made Variety of the First Type U.S. Army Distinguished Service Cross." *The Medal Collector* 24 (June 1973): 8-11 (ill).

Till, Paul H. "The Evolution of American Military Medals - An Initial Survey." *The Medal Collector* 29 (January 1978): 8-20.

Till, Paul H. "The Lincoln Pallbearers' Medals of Honor." *The Medal Collector* 20 (May 1969): 14-15.

Till, Paul H. "The 27th Maine Regiment - Those Who Remained." *The Medal Collector* 19 (November 1968): 34-38.

Till, Paul H. "Numbered U.S. Armed Forces Awards." *The Medal Collector* 22 (February 1971): 22-24.

Till, Paul H. "The Numbered U.S. Army Good Conduct Medal." *The Medal Collector* 22 (February 1971): 21-22.

Till, Paul H. "The Serial Numbering of American Medals - A Practice That Long Outlived Its Usefulness." *The Medal Collector* 31 (October 1980): 30-31.

Till, Paul H. "United States Army Awards." *The Medal Collector* 22 (June 1971): 15-25.

Till, Paul H. "U.S. Federal Reserve Service Medals and Ribbons." *The Medal Collector* 33 (March 1982): 14-15.

"Tinsel and Ribbon." *Time* 43 (January 24, 1944): 66.

"United States Navy Achievement Medal." *The Medal Collector* 19 (December 1968): 33.

Van Natter, F.M. "Story of the Purple Heart; Military Decoration Inaugurated by George Washington." *National Republic* 22 (September 1934): 3-4 (ill).

Wason, Alfred B. "Navy Gold Cross Medal of Honor World War I, April 1917 - November 1918." *The Medal Collector* 29 (January 1978): 22-24 (ill).

Wensyel, James W. "The Badge of Military Merit." *American History Illustrated* 17 (May 1982): 26-31; 46.

Werlich, Robert. "The Strange Case of Dr. Mary Walker." *The Medal Collector* 20 (June 1960): 21-38 (ill).

"Wheeler to Receive First DDS Medal." *The Medal Collector* 23 (February 1971): 20.

Williams, Dion. "War Decorations." *United States Naval Institute Proceedings* 45 (April 1919): 492-535 (ill).

Witnik, Ray A. "Commendation Medals." *The Medal Collector* 12 (November 1961): 12-15.

Wolfe, Bernard. "These Are the Badges of Courage: Our Soldiers and Sailors Now May Win Seventeen New Decorations and Service Medals." *Popular Science* 143 (July 1943): 56-60 (ill).

"World War Medals and a Newly Discovered Hero." *Literary Digest* 77 (June 23, 1923): 54-56.

Wyllie, Robert E. "Romance of Military Insignia: How the United States Government Recognizes Deeds of Heroism and Devotion to Duty." *National Geographic* 36 (December 1919): 463-450 (ill).

"You Can Trace the Fighter's Record by the Ribbons on His Chest." *Newsweek* 22 (October 11, 1943): 56-57 (ill).

[redacted]